Contents

STORY SUNDAY

Christian Fairy Tales for Young and Old Alike

John Aurelio

CROSSROAD • NEW YORK

1992

The Crossroad Publishing Company
370 Lexington Avenue, New York, NY 10017

Illustrations: Lonnie Sue Johnson

Printed in the United States of America

Library of Congress Cataloging-in-Publication Data

Aurelio, John.
    Story Sunday : Christian fairy tales for young and old alike /
John Aurelio ; illustrations, Lonnie Sue Johnson.
        p.   cm.
    Originally published: New York : Paulist Press, © 1978.
    Summary: A collection of fairy tales illustrating Christian
principles.
    ISBN 0-8245-1023-2 (pbk.)
    1. Fairy tales—United States.   2. Children's stories, American.
[1. Fairy tales.   2. Short stories.   3. Christian life—Fiction.]
I. Johnson, Lonnie Sue, ill.   II. Title.
[PZ8.A9246St   1992]
[Fic]—dc20   91–43515
                                                        CIP
                                                        AC

*To all of us
who in one way
or another
are "mentally retarded"*

Foreword

It was an exceptionally hot Sunday in July. I had just finished celebrating Mass with the retarded residents of the West Seneca Developmental Center and was hurrying over to St. Catherine's for the eleven o'clock Mass. This was held in the old town hall, a small New England churchlike building that housed the parish while the new church was under construction. I knew it would be hot and cramped inside.

"Good morning, Father," Joe waved as he quickly ushered me to a reserved parking spot near the door. "It's a real scorcher today and there's a full house inside. You'd better make it quick."

"Thanks for the tip," I called back as I opened the door. Inside it was like the mob scene from Cecil B. DeMille's *The Ten Command-ments*. The small room was crammed with disgruntled Israelites. Some few privileged ones were seated on folding chairs while many, many others shuffled restlessly along the walls, around the back and even down the center aisle. The children fidgeted restlessly, mana-cled in place by parental arms, stern looks and stage whisper calls to "sit still and shut up!" They were like a mob held in place by some unforeseen force in front of them. The makeshift altar rail was the Red Sea. As they parted ranks to let me pass, I knew how Moses felt when his people cried out to him, "Did you bring us out to this desert to die?"

To the side of the altar on a card table securely behind the altar rail lay the vestments. I vested with my side to the people, too nervous to face them directly but occasionally glancing sideways, wondering what I should do. A little child seated on its mother's lap caught me peeking. She raised her tiny hand and wiggled her fingers in greeting. I was beginning to raise mine in return when her father reached over and forced her hand down. "Sit still," he ordered. The incident totally distracted me from my worries about my homily, the time, the heat and the restless crowd. For the first time in years I glanced at the congregation noticing how many children there were. They were everywhere. But wherever they were, they were in captivity. Those who were standing were either encircled in a parent's arms or clasped firmly by the hand. Even those who were seated fared no better. They were kept in place by hands grasping their thighs or parental heads that moved like metronomes keeping them under constant surveillance.

"Set my children free," a voice called in my head.

"It's 'Set my people free'," I corrected.

"I know what I'm saying," the voice shot back.

It's precisely at times like this that unusual things begin to happen to me. I could hear the Lord calling out to me so I hurried away to the altar to begin the Mass, calling back to Him, "Please, send my brother Aaron."

I was at peace, even if an uneasy peace, when I sat down for the service of the Word. He was waiting for me.

"Set my children free."

"I know."

"Well?"

"Isn't the quote, 'Suffer the children to come unto me'," I said trying to change the subject.

"My children are suffering."

"I know. It's hot. We're all hot."

Silence.

"Okay, okay," I continued, "but if you want me to do what I think you want me to do, it's crazy. It won't work. Besides, I'm afraid."

"I will be with you."

When I finished the Gospel reading, I bowed in prayer before the altar, then turned to face the throng. "My friends. Today I am not going to preach my homily to you." There were audible sighs of relief. I felt that if they could have, they would have applauded. "Instead, I'm going to preach to the children." Looks of relief changed to disbelief. Before they could gather themselves into a formidable foe, I quickly continued. "It has just struck me that everything on Sunday is geared to adults. Is it any wonder the kids are restless? They have no reason to want to come to church."

There was a fearful silence. Behind me I could feel the threatening waters of the Red Sea. In front of my outstretched arms was the grumbling Israelite community and behind them the droning electric fans were the pharaoh's armies in hot pursuit.

"So today I'm going to ask the parents to sit quietly after they send the children up here to me. I'm going to tell them a story—a fairy tale!"

Their chains were broken. The children moved forward hesitatingly and sat down on the floor around me. There was no turning back now. "Lord save your people—and me too," I prayed as the room quieted down again.

"Once upon a time. . . ."

When the fairy tale was over I could see the confusion on the faces of the people. "The story is not without its Christian message," I continued after an agonizing pause. I was testing the waters warily. As quickly as I could I preached the moral.

It was over. I stood before them drenching wet with perspiration from head to toe. Had the sea behind me parted? I turned back to the altar. Then it happened. Slowly at first like a distant rumble gathering momentum. Then it burst forth and filled the room with its joyous sound. They were applauding. I was embarrassed.

That was the very first Story Sunday as it's become known to the people of St. Catherine's parish. It happened eight years ago. I never intended or even dreamed of repeating it again but our Lord and the people felt otherwise. At first I gave them only occasionally with just an announcement in the parish bulletin notifying the people in advance. But as the word spread others began to come from all over the city. To make it easier for the visitors and for the parish secretary, it was decided that the last Sunday of the month would be Story Sunday.

If this phenomenon, which, by the way, is not unique to us but seems to be growing everywhere, has anything to teach us it is that there is a definite need for such liturgies in the church. Our children need to feel a part of the worshipping community and not by bodily presence alone. Nor do I think that such children's liturgies should be held separate and apart from adult worship. With the growing fragmentation of the family in today's society, the church should be visibly in the forefront of keeping families together, especially at worship. An occasional liturgy directed toward children is not a serious hardship on adults. Not nearly as much as the reverse is for children.

When it finally impressed itself on my dense, Sicilian brain that Story Sunday would not go away, I began to search for stories that were applicable to preaching. Several of the traditional fairy tales with minor modifications (the villain never dies, or gets eaten up, or baked in an oven) are very adaptable to that purpose. Such stories as "The Ugly Duckling," "Beauty and the Beast," "The Midas Touch" and "The Fifty-First Dragon" are excellent for preaching Christian values. In time the parishioners themselves came to my aid supplying me with countless books, anthologies, and suggestions.

Eventually, inevitably I suppose, the well went dry.

That happened on Panic Saturday (the day before Story Sunday when I prepare the stories). I had one of my usual confrontations with the Lord.

"That's it! I can't find one."

Silence.

"Listen, Lord, I've spent the whole evening reading fairy tales. I've read German, Irish, Polish and even Grimm ones and I've gotten nothing but a headache. What do I do now?"

"My grace is sufficient."

"This is John, not Paul, you're talking to."

"I know who I'm talking to. Before you were formed in your mother's womb I knew you."

"Then you knew I would be stuck here. Remember this was your idea not mine. Your people are going to be there tomorrow and I don't have a story. What am I going to do?"

"My grace is sufficient."

"It figures. I'm going to take an aspirin. Maybe this whole thing will go away."

I took an aspirin and sat down in my Think Chair. I tried talking to the Lord again but He wouldn't communicate. Evidently not just His grace but His words were sufficient. I sulked and thought. Gradually, ever so gradually, but continuously, a story began to take shape. That was the first one. It was "The Magic Pill Man."

Since that time I have relied heavily on the Lord. His Word, and themes and problems of our times are the basis for my fairy tales.

What follows are some of those stories. I hope they provide the reader with entertainment, enlightenment and most important of all, the truth which is Jesus who is the Alpha and the Omega of them all.

* * * * *

Unfortunately, I am not gifted with a good memory. What I lack, God more than amply makes up for. To all who in any way helped me in my work, I sincerely thank you. God will remember your good works forever.

Introduction

The question arises: "How can one use these stories?" Perhaps the answer lies in their purpose—to entertain and to teach.

For those who feel that life is a mystery to be lived, I hope that the stories themselves afford some measure of entertainment. Each story taken as a whole presents a basic theological truth or moral. In telling these tales to children on Sunday it is this truth that I preach following the story. The format is identical to the parables of Jesus which are the models for Story Sunday. While the meaning behind the stories is aimed basically at adults, I have often found that children miss very little of it. I learned this when I did not preach after a particular story but instead told the children to ask their parents what it meant. This brought forth loud moans and laughter from the congregation and numerous phone calls to the rectory.

For those who feel that life is also a puzzle to be solved (I confess to be one of them) and who delight in discovering hidden meanings and disguised allusions, there should be ample grist for their mills in these stories. As the reader will discover, numerous persons, places and things are but symbols of other realities. The appendix will explain some but not all of these symbols. One should use the appendix only after personal deliberation and discovery. It is intended only as an aid for further discussion or where the symbolism is deliberately difficult as in "Johnny Crab and the Leprechaun."

Some of the stories are based on scriptural passages, for instance, "The Wart Princess," "The Peasant and the Princess" and "The Yellow Man". Each scriptural passage is printed in full because it is essential in understanding the story and setting the mood. Discussion afterward may then center around what the story has to do with the scripture.

Other stories are based on currents, trends, and problems in today's society. "The Magic Pill Man" and "Johnny Crab and the Leprechaun" were written as a reflection on specific issues facing

Christians today. "The Greatest Feat" is an overview of twentieth century man.

"The Parable" stands in a class by itself. It was written in the exact same style and format as are the parables of Jesus. It was delivered at the funeral of a thirteen year old boy, Anthony Frank. It speaks for itself.

Finally, I have for a long time harbored the great desire to do something to Christianize Christmas once again. The two great traditions of Christmas today are almost totally secular. I refer to Santa Claus and Dickens' *A Christmas Carol*. "The Best Christmas Gift of All" subtitled "A Story of Santa and the Christ Child" is my feeble attempt to link in children's minds Santa Claus and the reason for his existence, Jesus. *The Beggars' Christmas* (soon to be published under separate cover) is an unmistakably Christian Christmas carol.

There you have it—Story Sunday. May it give you as much joy and less anguish than it has given me over the years. As for me, I have fought the good fight. I have finished the race. . . .

"John, that's Paul."

"I know, Lord. I know."

God's peace,
Father John

THE WART PRINCESS

"When the unclean spirit departs from a man, it roams through arid wastes searching for a place of rest and finding none. Then it says, "I will go back where I came from," and returns to find the dwelling unoccupied, though swept and tidied now. Off it goes again to bring back with it this time seven spirits more evil than itself. They move in and settle there. Thus the last state of that man becomes worse than the first. And that is how it will be with this evil generation" (Matthew 12:43-45).

Once upon a time, a long, long time ago, in the country of England far, far away, the King and Queen gave birth to a beautiful daughter named Gwendolyn. Princess Gwendolyn was so beautiful she was almost perfect. She had a pretty, round little face, a dimpled chin, big brown eyes and silky hair. She was almost perfect, except for one tiny flaw. At the tip of her cute little button nose there was a wart. A very tiny wart, a hardly noticeable wart. But none the less—a wart. The King was not concerned about it.

"Pay it no mind," he said to the Queen. "When she grows up, it will go away!"

But it didn't go away. Nor did it bother young Princess Gwendolyn. She was too busy having fun and playing games with other children of the palace to give any attention to the wart on her nose.

Even as she grew through adolescence and into young maidenhood, she was much too busy and much too happy to let a little wart distract her. Her time was always filled with things to do. When the royal physician would leave the castle to tend a sick villager, Princess Gwendolyn would always accompany him and help care for his patient. Whenever there was a festival, the Princess would join in with the people—sit and eat at table with them—share their food, drink their wine. She would dance and sing and party with them never thinking it beneath her station. All the people of the kingdom loved her. No one even noticed the wart at the tip of her nose.

One day when the King had returned from a visit with the King and Queen of France, he sent for his daughter, the Princess, for he had good news to tell her.

"What is it my Father?" she asked. "What news do you have that makes you so excited?"

"While I was in France visiting the castle of the King and Queen, I had the good fortune to meet their only son, Prince Jacques. He was such a fine and handsome young man. Everything about him was appealing. He was a valiant soldier, an excellent hunter and an exceptional scholar. Everyone I spoke to thought most highly of him."

"Yes," Gwendolyn said excitedly, guessing now at what the good news was. "Yes?"

"Did I tell you what a fine figure of a man he was?" her father teased, "that he's tall and ruddy and strong as a bull?"

"Yes father, you did. But tell me what you called me for or I shall burst," she cried.

Laughing at her excitement and unable to contain his news any longer, he proclaimed, "I have made arrangements for the two of you to be wed. You are to be married in one year's time—the summer next. He will sail here from France and wed you in the Castle Church. It will be a wedding the likes of which the world has never seen. England and France will be joined in Gwendolyn and Jacques."

The Princess almost burst with joy when her father told her what she'd suspected. Handsome Prince Jacques. She had heard much about the young Prince—of his courage as a soldier, of his valor and his kindness. And yes, she had many times heard the young women of the castle speak of his very handsome face. To think he was to be her husband.

The Queen broke into her reverie. "We must make haste. Everything must be made ready for such a great wedding of state."

The whole kingdom was aflutter making preparations for the great day. The royal chef planned the meal, the ladies-in-waiting planned the ball, the archbishop planned the ceremony, even the townspeople, who loved the Princess so much, prepared to decorate their homes.

When the royal dressmaker came to show the Princess the lace he was going to use for her bridal veil, she was thrilled at the fineness and the beauty of it. She placed it ever so gently over her hair and gazed into the mirror. "It is beautiful," she thought. However, as she looked into the mirror her smile began to fade. For the first time in a long while she noticed the wart at the end of her nose.

"Such an unbecoming thing," she said to herself. "I must get rid of it before the wedding."

She quickly took some powder and powdered her nose but still it showed. She rubbed some ointment over it to try to conceal it, but she couldn't.

"What can I do about this terrible wart? How can a princess with a wart on her nose marry a handsome prince? I must get rid of this horrible wart."

The Princess immediately sent for the royal physician. "You

11

must do something about this," she said pointing to her nose. "You must rid me of this wart," she commanded.

"I will try," replied the physician who returned to his quarters where he began at once to prepare medications. Alas! Every medicine he tried failed. Try he did, over and over again, but nothing would remove the wart.

"You must try harder," screamed the Princess. "The wedding is drawing nearer."

"But your Highness," pleaded the physician, "I have done all that I can. There are villagers who are sick and they have need of me. I must go to them."

"NO!" shouted the Princess. "You must help me first. You may not leave the castle until this wart is gone." The royal guards then came and took the physician back to his rooms where they kept guard over him so that he could not leave.

The Princess then sent for her father's counselors—including the royal chef and royal tailor.

"You are the wisest men of the kingdom. Tell me, what must be done to rid me of this wart?" None would dare speak for now they were all afraid. The royal chef stepped forward.

"Speak!" the Princess commanded.

"I hear tell that many blemishes are caused by improper diet. I once visited a chef in another kingdom who told me how he prepared a special drink for his ailing king whose body was covered with sores. A period of time after the king drank the brew his skin healed, becoming clear again."

"Make me this drink," shouted Gwendolyn.

"It takes much to do it, my Princess. One must bring in a great deal of food, fruits and vegetables, then squeeze them under a press to make but a little cupful of the drink."

"I would have it," she screamed. So she ordered the soldiers to go through the kingdom and bring in all the fruits and vegetables and whatever other good food there was to the royal chef.

The poor villagers. They had lost their physician and now their food was being taken away from them. But they could do nothing or say nothing.

The chef made his special drink over and over again, but still the

12

wart remained at the end of the Princess' nose.

Again she called in the counselors.

"I will have you all thrown into the dungeon unless you give me wise counsel." She waited. They consulted among themselves for a long while until, finally, the royal tailor came up with a suggestion.

"Your Highness," he said timidly, "The wart is truly no big thing, but it so distracts your attention. What I suggest is that you wear the prettiest clothes in the land, clothes of the finest wool and cotton with threads spun of silver and gold. You will be so dazzling in appearance, no one will ever notice such a tiny insignificant wart."

"Make them for me," she cried. Thus all the wool and cotton of the land were brought to the castle leaving the villagers and townsfolk throughout the country with nothing to use to make their own clothes. Nor did the Princess care. She had to do it, she felt, because of her wart.

When at last the seamstresses presented her with a wardrobe the likes of which the world had never seen, the Princess made haste to try her beautiful outfits on. She tried on one garment after another, but each time, when she looked in the mirror, all she could see was the wart at the end of her nose.

"Can no one help me?" she screamed.

Fearing lest they be thrown in the castle dungeon, the counselors suggested that she see the village sorcerer. Off she went in a bound.

"My Lady," he said. "One does not know what wisdom will come from this cauldron. But, I am sure there is an answer here."

So he prepared his brew until the pot boiled and bubbled. Then, taking a little scraping from the Princess' wart, he put that into the pot. At once the cauldron began to smoke. The sorcerer stared into the smoke, watching intently. At last he said, "The answer is, my Princess, that you must give it away."

"What manner of answer is that?" she shouted. "If I could give it away, I would. But how do I do that?"

"One may not question any further; your answer has been given."

"Give it away," thought the Princess. "I see. I understand now."

She hurried home and issued a proclamation which was read throughout the length and breadth of the kingdom.

"Hear Ye, Hear Ye—by decree of her Royal Highness, Princess Gwendolyn, all people of the kingdom must have a wart at the end of their noses. Anyone who does not comply will be thrown in the castle dungeon. Hear ye, Hear Ye."

So it was that all the people of the kingdom did whatever they could to grow warts at the end of their noses. Those who couldn't, painted one on which was just as good.

"Now that everyone has a wart," said Gwendolyn, "no one will notice mine."

So she mounted her horse and began riding through the kingdom. There were warts everywhere. Everywhere she looked, all the people had warts at the end of their noses. But instead of helping her to forget her wart, seeing all the rest of them made her more and more conscious of her own.

She could stand it no longer. She could not bear to see another wart. She must hurry back to the castle and hide away in her room. She turned back to the castle riding at lightning speed. While she rode, the wind began to blow and the skies darkened. The clouds opened and a driving rain poured down on the countryside. Lightning flashed everywhere and the sound of thunder filled the air. The Princess' horse became frightened and bolted so that she fell to the ground. Wet and muddy, she looked for a place to find shelter.

There, in the woods, she could see smoke rising from the chimney of a small cottage. She hurried there and knocked on the door. The old peasant man who opened the door was surprised to see anyone out on such a terrible night.

"Come in, my child. Come in and get warm by the fire."

The Princess was chilled and shivering as she sat near the fire. She was crying, too. Crying that all her hopes and plans were ruined because of an ugly wart. The old man believed she was upset because of the cold and her wet clothes.

"Don't cry, my child. I will find something dry for you to wear. Although heaven knows where I will find it."

He went searching around his poor hut all the while talking to the shivering girl.

"It's so hard these days. I can't make clothes anymore because the Wart Princess has taken all our cotton and wool. But don't worry, I'm sure I can find something."

14

"Wart Princess?" asked Gwendolyn. "Who's the Wart Princess?"

"That's Princess Gwendolyn," he replied not knowing whom he was talking to.

"The King's daughter. She once was a wonderful maiden, but the people fear that an evil spirit has her now, and she has punished the people in her wickedness."

Gwendolyn sat there stunned. From Fair Gwendolyn to the Wart Princess. She began to cry harder.

"What you need," the old man continued rambling, "is a good vegetable broth. It would warm you and take away the chill. But alas, we have no vegetables either. The Wart Princess has taken them all for herself."

"This, too, I have done," thought Gwendolyn. And her tears were as numerous as the raindrops that fell outside.

"You must not cry," said the old man. "You will make yourself sick. And if you get sick, there is no physician to help you, for he was locked up in the castle dungeon by the Wart Princess."

"Enough," cried Gwendolyn. "Enough! I can't stand to hear any more." She ran out of the little hut and all the way back to the castle.

"What have I done?" she cried as she entered the castle. "For the sake of a wart, I have become a wicked person."

"No longer," she cried out as she ran to the dungeon and released the physician. Next she ordered the guards to return all the food and cloth to the villagers and pay them double, no, triple, in gold for all that she took.

When this was all done, the Princess herself went to every home in the kingdom to tell the people she was sorry. Those who had painted warts on their noses, she, herself, cleaned them off. Those who had grown warts she personally kissed, and as she did, the warts disappeared. When she was finished, all the warts in the kingdom were gone. All that is, but one—hers.

When at last her wedding day arrived and Prince Jacques entered the courtyard on his gallant steed, all the townspeople assembled to see the handsome Prince and the soon-to-be Bride. Princess Gwendolyn dressed in fine clothes, bowed low before the Prince, and held her hand over her nose trying for as long as possible not to have him see her ugly wart. The Prince dismounted and took her hand from her

15

face, and bowed low to kiss it. Curious to see the handsome Prince, Gwendolyn lifted her eyes ever so slightly, just as his lips touched the back of her hand. She could not believe her eyes. For there, at the end of his princely nose, in plain view for all to see . . . . .was a wart!

THE GREATEST FEAT

Once upon a time, a long, long time ago, there was a great and mighty king. The kingdom he ruled was so big, extended so far beyond what any man had ever seen, that they called him the King of the Universe.

One day he sent a royal proclamation to be read in all the villages and towns throughout the kingdom:

"HEAR YE, HEAR YE!
EVERYONE EVERYWHERE—
HIS SUPREME MAJESTY DECREES:

I WILL GIVE MY ENTIRE KINGDOM—
THE LENGTH AND BREADTH,
THE HEIGHT AND DEPTH—
TO THE PERSON
WHO PERFORMS THE GREATEST FEAT."

One can imagine the excitement the royal decree caused among the people. It was rumored that the king had no heir and this undoubtedly meant he was in search of one. How great the feat would have to be to inherit such a kingdom. What marvelous feats would be performed for the king before he would make his judgment.

When the day arrived for the competition to begin, people flocked to the king's castle from the four corners of the earth. Wizards, sorcerers, jugglers, acrobats, scholars, magicians, musicians. They were all there in endless numbers and countless varieties. Into the courtyard they poured—a steady stream that grew into a river until the yard was filled to overflowing.

At last the king's minister appeared at the balcony that overlooked the assembled throng. He tapped his staff solemnly, reverently, three times on the stone floor. The sound of trumpet blasts filled the air, calling the crowds to silence and heralding the imminent presence of the king. All eyes looked to the balcony.

The King of the Universe appeared. The crowd fell to utter silence. It was as if the ponderous weight of his awesome majesty had suddenly been felt by the crowd as it stooped under the magnitude of it. He sat.

The minister tapped his staff and announced, "Let the competition begin."

For many long hours jugglers juggled, acrobats tumbled and musicians played. Everyone who wished to compete was given the opportunity to perform. The king and his retinue sat silently in the balcony observing carefully all that took place below.

Day followed upon day until nearly everyone had performed. When the last contestant was finishing his feat, a murmuring began in the crowd. As it spread through the people, it gained intensity until it

18

was no longer a whisper but a shout: "THE WIZARDS HAVE ARRIVED."

Everyone turned to the castle gate. As the four wizards entered, the crowds shouted and cheered in a wild frenzy. They had become tired of watching similar feats over and over again and yearned for something exciting and spectacular. Certainly the wizards would satisfy this craving for no one could perform the marvelous deeds they could. The only real competition should have been between them, but the king had insisted that everyone who wanted to perform could try. So the wizards waited until the end as if to save the best until last.

It was the Wizard of the North who came forward first. He was a tall and stately man of regal bearing. He would make a fine heir to the king. He was dressed in a long flowing robe of pitch black that covered his entire body. His face and hands, the only parts of him that were uncovered, were a pure and dazzling white. Slowly he walked through the assembly, stood before the balcony, and bowed. The crowds watched with absolute reverential silence.

Without a word, the Wizard of the North reached into a pouch which hung at his waist and withdrew from it a handful of powder. With a long, deliberate gesture, he threw the powder into the air. It immediately began to sparkle in the sunlight like a million brilliant diamonds. The people watched in awe as the powder rose steadily higher, progressively faster, until it became a comet and burst into the sun in a dazzling explosion of white light.

At first the people were filled with fear, covering their faces against the blinding flash. Then a voice cried out, "Look! Look around you everybody!" The scene they opened their eyes to was a very strange one indeed. The world had become a stark contrast of black and white. The buildings that were light had suddenly become a brilliant, eye-squinting white. The buildings that were dark had become dense black. The same was true for the animals. Dark ones were black and light ones were white. It was on people, however, that it had the most peculiar effect. If they were light, their hands and faces became dazzling white. If they were dark, the bodies appeared deep black. The clothes they wore took on the same peculiar quality so that people looked like checkerboard patches of contrasting black and white. In truth, the world had become black and white.

The people, overwhelmed by such wizardry, began to shout and applaud with delight.

"Surely this must be the greatest feat. No one has ever seen the likes of this. The Wizard of the North should win the prize."

Seated in his balcony, the king remained silent. The wizard bowed obediently before the king, and everything returned to the way it was before.

The Wizard of the South then stepped forward. He was an old man with white hair and a long white beard. Instead of a staff as a walking stick, he carried a sickle. He bowed slightly but reverently before the King of the Universe. Again the crowds became silent.

Ever so slowly the wizard raised his right arm and with a bony finger pointed at the steeple clock. All heads were raised. All eyes looked to the clock. Deliberately, very deliberately, the wizard began to move his finger in a circle. As his finger moved so did the hands of the clock. At first the movement was so slow that people wondered what the wizard might be drawing their attention to. Gradually they began to notice what was happening. With each rotation of his finger, an hour would pass on the steeple clock. His finger moved faster. The clouds began to accelerate. Animals and people began to move more quickly. Shadows changed rapidly. Even the way people spoke was high pitched and peculiarly fast. Still the wizard moved his finger in a circle faster and faster. Time now began to fly by. In an instant the sun would rise, clouds streak across the sky; then it would rain and become dry in the batting of an eye; next the wind would blow and abate as quickly as a breath; then the sun would set only to rise again moments later and the same phenomenon would repeat itself.

When everything was moving as fast as time and imagination would allow, the wizard began to slow down the movement of his finger. The sun's trajectory, the clouds' progression, the earth's hectic pace began to diminish and become more normal. The people breathed easier, their voices became intelligible again.

The wizard stood there in the courtyard still pointing to the clock, still moving his finger slower and slower until it seemed that time had all but stopped. The sun was a fixed light in the sky that burned unbearably hot on an immobile world. All movement slowed to a labored infinitesimal progression. Once again speech was incomprehensible because of the length of time it took each word to be formed and uttered. The falling of a leaf took an eternity. Nothing changed, nothing seemed to move except the wizard's finger. Up it moved, up in weighted effort until it reached the summit; once beyond the drag of gravity the finger moved in descent with increasing momentum until at last, time returned to normal.

A deafening cheer rose from the crowd. Never had anyone experienced such a remarkable feat. The king must surely name the Wizard of the South as his heir.

Seated in his balcony, the king remained silent. The Wizard of the South bowed to the king and left the courtyard. The competition was not yet over. The Wizard of the East was about to perform.

The wizard had no sooner entered the gate when the people began to cry out in amazement. As he walked, the wizard changed. He passed beyond the castle gate walking straight and tall as a young, strong man. After several paces, his gait slowed, and before their eyes, he became a doddering old man. As he continued toward the balcony, he changed again into a beautiful young maiden whose steps became as graceful as those of a ballerina. The ballerina twirled and jumped into the air becoming a young child as her feet touched ground again. A few skips and some hops and the wizard stood before the king as a stately and mature man.

The crowds were overwhelmed. They laughed and applauded with each change the wizard made. If this was just his entrance, imagine his performance. The wizard raised his arms to silence them.

"Bring me some fruit," he ordered. A vendor nearby with a basket full of apples in the crook of his arm stepped forward. The wizard took the basket and placed it on the ground before him. With great ceremony he raised his two arms and waved his hands over the apples. When he finished, there were no longer apples before him, but big, green watermelons. The crowd responded with shouts of delight. The wizard ordered the vendor to sell his new fruit to the crowds. As the people ate the watermelons, they began to shout with laughter. The watermelons, although they looked and felt like watermelons, tasted just like apples. The discovery delighted the people.

The commotion of the crowd caused a dog to start barking with excitement.

"Bring the dog here," the wizard commanded.

A young boy led the reluctant barking dog by the collar to where the wizard was standing. The wizard ceremoniously waved his arms over the frightened animal. In an instant, in place of the dog, there stood a cat with the exact same color and markings as the dog . . . but none the less, a cat. The crowd watched with quiet amazement. The animal, confused by the change and sudden silence, opened its mouth in protest. However, instead of meowing as one would expect, the cat began to bark. At first the people were startled by the unexpected turn of events. Then they became hysterical with laughter at the sight of a cat barking and growling in frenzy.

The boy looked at the wizard pleadingly. The wizard waved his arms over the boy, and in an instant, the boy became a beautiful young maiden. Once again the feat brought everyone to silence including the barking cat. The maiden who stood there with long, golden hair and red ruby lips was the most beautiful woman the kingdom had ever seen. The boy made maiden looked at his dog made cat and called out to him in a voice quite unmistakably masculine. At that, the frightened cat began to bark; the crowd roared with laughter; and the maiden cried with a man's voice.

The wizard raised his arms over the scene and waved them solemnly. The maiden changed back to the boy, the cat became a barking dog again, and the people were holding apples and not watermelons.

Thunderous applause echoed throughout the castle walls. Never had the world seen such a feat. The Wizard of the East would win the throne.

The king remained silent. The contest was not over yet. The wizard bowed and walked away.

The Wizard of the West now entered the courtyard. As the crowd made way to let him pass, they were struck by the peculiar robe the wizard wore. The robe was covered with mirrors, hundreds of mirrors of different sizes and shapes. Mirrors that hung down in front and cascaded down his back. Mirrors on his sleeves, and shoes and in his hair. Mirrors on his wizard's hat. As he walked the mirrors tinkled against one another as an oriental chime does in the breeze. As he bowed before the King of the Universe, it seemed as if every person in the courtyard was reflected in his mirrors.

He turned to the hushed crowd.

22

"You have seen great feats performed before you. Now, I shall perform the greatest of them all."

In a solemn voice that all could hear, the wizard said, "Ask of me anything!"

The announcement startled the people. They had seen so many marvelous feats by the other wizards, that they could not suddenly think of their individual needs and desires. As they began to ponder his words, and in the light of the miracles they had witnessed, they began to think of the spectacular, of the astounding things they could ask him to do. A voice cried out from the crowd, "Make us fly."

Quite unlike other wizards, without any hesitation, without any ceremony, he clapped his hands and announced, "YOU CAN FLY."

Cautiously, suspiciously, they listened to what he said but no one moved.

"You can fly," he repeated matter-of-factly.

Finally, someone began to beat his arms in the air, like a bird with wings, testing to see if the wizard spoke the truth. In a moment he was in the air flying. The others looked in amazement. They too began to flap their arms in happy anticipation. Soon everyone was in the air, young and old, man and woman, flying and soaring above the castle courtyard. Only the wizard remained on the ground. All the flying people were reflected in his countless mirrors.

When the excitement of their flying had passed, they returned to the courtyard to see what other marvelous things the Wizard of the West would do for them. Someone cried out, "Let there be music and dancing."

"So be it," said the wizard as he clapped his hands.

All kinds of musical instruments appeared. Curiously the people picked them up and began to play. Flutes, harps, oboes, horns, clarinets, trumpets, pianos; instruments of every kind. Without ever having had a lesson the people began to play. Happy, beautiful music filled the air while people laughed and danced for hours.

"We are hungry now; we want food."

"As you wish," said the wizard.

There before them were large banquet tables covered with every kind of food they had ever heard or dreamed of. Some people ate and drank, while others of them danced, others made music and still others flew in the sky. All of this was reflected in the wizard's mirrors.

Finally, people began asking for possessions for themselves.

"Give me jewels," and at once they had jewels.

"Give me a farm," and there in the courtyard was a farm.

"Give me horses."

"Give me cows."

"Give me pigs."

"Give me money," and at once the courtyard began to fill with the growing demands of the people.

On and on they asked as the courtyard filled to overflowing with houses, carriages, clothes, animals, an endless variety of different things. People could no longer move because there were so many things, so much confusion.

In the midst of the tables filled with goodies, in the midst of the yard filled with whining and bleating animals, a young man stood, calling loudly to make himself heard above the din of the crowd. He tried pushing his way forward to where the wizard was, but the crowds would not let him pass, for they still had needs that they shouted to the wizard. The young man tried harder to move forward but all his attempts were thwarted. When he began to kick over the tables to make headway, he infuriated many in the crowd. After all, these were their gifts that the wizard had given them. He had no right to destroy them. In a fury they turned on him and struck him down. The degree of their own violence surprised them. The incident took but a moment; it was unpleasant, but over. The people turned back to the wizard, continuing to shout their requests.

The King's minister rose and walked to the edge of the balcony. He solemnly tapped three times with his staff then all became quiet. The King rose from his throne and looked down at the courtyard below him. The contest was over.

His voice was calm but powerful as he addressed the people.

"Who, say you, performed the greatest feat?"

"The Wizard of the West," they shouted in reply. How quickly they had forgotten the others. It was unanimous. The Wizard of the West should be the heir and inherit the kingdom.

"Not the Wizard of the West," announced the King to the crowds' bewilderment. They felt that he certainly had performed the greatest feats.

24

The King of the Universe continued, "the Wizard of the West gave the people everything they wanted, everything they asked for. Truly that was great, but he took the struggle out of life. By so doing, he took the meaning out of life. No, not the Wizard of the West."

There was a quiet pause in the crowd as they gathered their recollections.

"The Wizard of the East," they clamored. Since he was the next to the last, he was the next remembered.

"Not the Wizard of the East," replied the King. "True, his feats were marvelous, but he made things change. He made things appear to be what they were not. He took the truth out of life."

The silence lasted longer. Some voices cried out, "The Wizard of the South".

"Not the Wizard of the South either. He could control time. However, when he made the time pass quickly, the young were happy but the old were sad. When the time moved slowly, the young were sad and the old happy. He stole the meaning of time from life."

From those who could still remember the suggestion came, "The Wizard of the North."

"Not the Wizard of the North. He made the world and everything in it black and white. He took the color out of life. He took the beauty out of life. Not the Wizard of the North."

The people now were silenced into total bewilderment. Who then performed the greatest feat? Surely no one had done anything to equal what the wizards had done. Slowly, the people began to murmur and mumble. It was all a ruse. The King will not give away his kingdom. Their anger grew like the tide, rising higher and higher beating up against the castle walls.

"What greater feat can any man do than those which were performed by our wizards? There can be no greater feat," they shouted.

The King's minister struck his staff on the stone balcony floor. The crowd became silent.

"There was one among you," the King said solemnly, "who rose from the dead."

The news staggered the crowd. It was incredible. Rise from the dead? Impossible! No one had died during the contest. Or hadn't they noticed?

25

"Did anyone die?" they asked among themselves. The inquiry was repeated until those near the tables heard it. Embarrassed and ashamed, they remembered the struggle with the young man. They apologized for striking him down, claiming that in the confusion, they did not know what they were doing.

"Where is he now?" they asked. To everyone's amazement he was no longer there. Try as they might they could not find him anywhere. They looked . . . but he was gone.

The King repeated his statement, "There was one among you who rose from the dead. To him belongs my kingdom from the length to the breadth, from the height to the depth. I hereby further decree that anyone who finds him will share the kingdom with him forever."

Having said this, the King left the balcony and returned to the castle. The people in the courtyard hurried over to where the young man had been. Some of his friends had gathered there.

"What does he look like?" they asked. "How will we recognize him?" Slowly, the people left the courtyard. Out through the castle gates they left and returned to their homes telling everyone they met of the greatest feat.

THE MAGIC PILL MAN

Once upon a time, not very long ago or very far away there lived a young boy named John. He lived in a big house with a large porch and a huge chestnut tree right in front. On hot summer days when it was too hot to play games, John would sit beneath the tree with his back propped up against the trunk and watch the clouds make different pictures in the sky.

It was on one such day, while he was trying to make something of a peculiar cloud formation, that an odd looking man stepped in front of him. He was dressed all in black, like the chimney sweeps in London, except that he wore a top hat. Hanging from his shoulders by straps like suspenders was a small black tray filled with bottles of all sizes, colors and shapes.

"Who are you?," John asked.

"Why, I'm the magic pill man," he answered, a bit surprised that the boy did not know him.

"Is that what you've got in those bottles—pills?"

"Magic pills," the pill man replied. "Magic pills. All kinds of magic pills: all colors, all sizes and all shapes. I have pills that make you tall and pills that make you small. I have fat little pills that make you skinny and skinny little pills that make you fat. I have blue pills and green pills and pills of many other colors. There are square ones and round ones, and even some in the shape of animals and people." Each time he mentioned a different kind, he took the bottle with those pills from the tray, showed them to the boy, and very carefully replaced them.

"You mustn't get your pills confused, you know!"

"Where are you going with them?", John asked.

"Wherever I'm needed. I usually don't go too far because there are so many people who want me. If you want to see me work my magic, come along with me."

So the two of them went off, walking down the village street. They hadn't walked very far when they heard someone shouting, "Magic pill man, Magic pill man, Wait! I'll be right there."

John looked to see where the voice was coming from. He was startled when he found that the voice came from a house that was belching out smoke everywhere. Smoke came out of the doors, the windows, the chimney even from under the porch.

John shouted, "Quick, let's call the firemen." But before he could run off, the magic pill man grabbed him by the back of his pants and held him still.

"No need to do that, son," he said laughingly. "There's no fire there, just smoke. Besides, he's one of my best customers. Well, you wanted to see what magic my pills would do; now you'll see."

At that moment a man emerged from the smoking house. He

looked very odd because he walked out of the house backwards, flapping a towel that he held between his hands. He looked as if he were either fanning the fire or trying to blow away the smoke. John decided it was the latter, since the pill man said there was no fire.

"May I have one of my pills?" he said to the pill man without even noticing the boy.

"Certainly." The pill man reached into a smoke-colored bottle and gave him a grey pill which the man immediately popped into his mouth.

"Now watch the magic," the pill man whispered to John.

At that, the man's feet began to move faster and faster until they moved so fast that they were just a blur beneath him. Off he ran, faster then John had ever seen anyone run before. Into the house he ran with his towel flapping even faster than an electric fan. The man ran into a room, closed the door and opened the window. Then, with incredible speed, he waved and flapped the towel until all the smoke was blown out of the room. Then, as quick as a flash, he ran to the next room and did the same.

"That's wonderful," John said. "That's a wonderful pill."

"Yes it is, isn't it? But it's only good for that, you know. I have other pills for other things. Would you like to see how some of the others work?"

John was so excited with the new-found magic he could hardly wait. However, before they could leave, they heard the same voice call out again, "Magic pill man, Magic pill man, Wait!"

Once again the house was filled with smoke—smoke coming out of everywhere, just as before.

"What happened?" John asked the man.

"The pill began to wear out," he replied, "and as it did, I moved slower and slower until the house filled with smoke again."

Without paying any attention to the boy, he took another pill and was off again. The sight of the man frantically opening windows in one room after another made John double over with laughter. The smoke disappeared. But once again, as the pill started to wear off, he moved slower and slower and the house filled with smoke. Again he came out to ask the pill man for another pill.

This puzzled John so he said to the man, "That's no way to get rid

29

of the smoke. Why don't you just find out where it's coming from and get rid of that?"

"Why should I?" was his answer. "What do you know?" With that he took another pill and was off in a flash.

"That's silly," John said to the pill man.

The pill man merely said, "We'd better hurry off if you want to see more magic."

Next, they encountered an enormously fat lady like the one John had seen at the county fair last summer. In her hands she held a pretty blue and white gingham dress.

"Look," she cried to the magic pill man. "I want to wear this dress. Have you any pills that could help me?"

John politely kept himself from laughing because the dress was quite obviously many sizes too small for her. If the pill man could do something about that, it would indeed be magic.

This time he opened a bottle with the tiniest little round pills in it and gave one to the fat lady. The three of them stood there waiting for the longest time. Nothing happened. When the pill man saw John getting restless he whispered to him, "Sometimes it takes longer, especially if they have a bigger job to do."

At last the lady began to giggle with delight. "It's working," she cried, "it's working."

It was amazing, but she was beginning to get thinner right before their eyes. John's eyes were wide with surprise.

"I don't believe it; she's really getting skinny. Look at her."

But the pill man was too busy laughing and dancing to hear what he said.

"It's magic," Johnny shouted. "Wonderful magic." All three joined hands and danced in a circle.

At last, when she was thin enough, the fat lady put on the skinny dress, and it fit her perfectly. She danced and twirled, modeled her new dress for them to see.

"You can't imagine how badly I wanted to wear this dress. More than anything else in the world I wanted to wear this dress, and now it fits." She walked straight over to them.

Just as she got to them, a button popped. "Oh, my goodness," she cried, "I must get my needle and thread." Before she could reach into her bag, another button popped and then another. She was getting bigger again.

"Quick, give me another pill."

Back into the bottle he reached and gave her another small pill.

Once again her size began to shrink so the buttons stopped popping.

"I must find my needle and thread. You see, I must wear this dress. I just must wear this dress."

However, it took her so long to find them that she was again getting way too fat for the dress to fit.

"Quick, give me another pill before more buttons pop," she cried.

As the pill man went back to his bottles John said to the lady, "If you want to wear that dress so much, why don't you just get a bigger one?"

"Why should I?" she replied. "Besides, you're just a young boy. What do you know?" Once more she took another pill.

John was tired and said to the pill man, "This is silly. Let's go." But he was so startled and frightened by the next person or persons they encountered that he forgot he was tired. It or he was a very tall, three-headed man, a giant really. If it weren't for his curiosity, Johnny probably would have run off. But the giant seemed gentle enough. Never in his life, not even in his dreams, had he ever before seen a three-headed man. And three such peculiar heads they were. One, the one on the left, was fast asleep and snoring soundly. The other one on the right was wide awake with eyes like saucers staring out. The head in the middle continually turned back and forth between the other two heads saying, "My, oh my, oh my!"

"Pill man," the middle head said, "you must give me some pills. Oh my, Oh my, Oh my!"

"Certainly", the pill man answered, "Three different pills for three different heads. Now remember, wake up the head on the left just long enough for him to swallow the square pill; the head on the right gets the round one. Then, when the one on the left is really awake and the one on the right goes to sleep give the head on the left the round pill and wake up the head on the right just long enough for him to swallow the square one. Then, when the head on the right is

31

really awake, he gets the round one and the head on the left must wake up just long enough to swallow another square one. Do you have that straight, now?"

"What about me?" said the head in the middle in a muddle. "I have to do all the work. Don't you have any pill for me?"

"Yes, there's one for you too," said the pill man as he reached into a different bottle and took out a pill that moved and squiggled like a Mexican jumping bean.

When John got over his shock and fear, he worked up enough courage to ask the giant what he was doing.

"This head here," the giant answered, "the one on my left that's sleeping, he gets the square pill I think? Yes, the square pill. That will keep him sleeping for a while."

"Why do you want him to sleep?" the boy asked.

"You're young. What do you know? Oh my, Oh my, Oh my. One has to stay asleep because as everybody knows, two's company, three's a crowd. Oh my, Oh my, Oh my. I thought everyone knew that."

"What about the other head?" John continued. "What's his pill for?"

"To keep him awake, naturally. One other head always has to stay awake."

"Why?"

"Oh, my, Oh my, Oh my. Because two heads are better than one. I thought everyone knew that."

"Then why do you need a pill?"

"For my nerves, boy! For my nerves. I have to remember which head stays awake and which one goes to sleep, and who takes the square pill, and who gets the round one. My nerves are shot I tell you. My nerves are shot trying to keep all this straight."

John was beginning to tire of his excursion. He wasn't too impressed with the magic pills either. The magic pill man must have sensed it when he said to John "I've saved the best till last. Wait till you see this next magic pill at work."

The path they were walking on led them directly to a high stone wall with a large iron gate locked shut. Sitting on the ground at the foot of the wall was a young man. He was crying. When he saw the pill man, his face lit up with joy. He jumped up and ran over to them.

"You're here. At last you're here. I've been waiting so long."

The pill man turned to John, "Now I know you're going to like this one. All young people do."

He reached into a bottle and gave the young man an odd-shaped pill. In one quick motion, the young man took the pill and popped it into his mouth.

John watched intently. He stared and stared as the young man's arms started to move. Up and down. Up and down. Faster and faster till they were moving so quickly that the young man began to rise off the ground. The more he flapped his arms, the higher into the air he went. He was flying! John could hear the young man laughing and shouting with excitement as he flew like a bird. He flew in circles and loops. He'd come swooping down and just as quickly, soar into the sky again.

"That's wonderful," said John. "Now that's magic."

"I knew you'd like it," said the pill man.

It was wonderful to watch the young man. He was as young people should be: happy, carefree, flying high. John could barely stand still from excitement. At last, this was a pill he wanted.

He was just about to ask for one from the pill man, when he noticed the young man's voice had changed.

"It's wearing off," he cried. "It's wearing off. Don't go!"

Down he came, back to the ground. He slumped at the foot of the wall crying.

"I didn't make it again," he cried.

John walked over to the young man.

"What do you mean you didn't make it?" he asked.

"I want to get over the wall," the young man said, "but every time I start to fly, I get so excited and happy I forget where I want to go. Then, I always fall back down on this side of the wall."

"You mean, you have tried before?" John asked.

"Many times," he answered, "and it's always the same."

"If you want to get over the wall," John said, "why don't you just climb over it? It's not too high."

"Why should I? It's more fun to fly," he said as he returned to the pill man for another pill.

"This is silly," John thought. "This whole thing is silly. Little round pills for fat people, square pills to make you sleep, odd-shaped pills for flying. They're not real magic; they're foolish." He turned away then, and walked home.

"John! John!" he heard his mother's voice calling to him.

"Yes, Mom, what do you want?"

"Time to eat, hurry upstairs and wash."

"All right." The screen door slammed shut behind him. Slowly he walked up the stairs thinking to himself: remembering the fat lady, the three-headed giant, the young boy. They were really foolish, he thought. Why did they ever take those silly pills?

Just as he reached the bathroom door, he heard his mother's voice call up from the kitchen, "And don't forget to take your vitamin pill before dinner!"

THE PARABLE

Once upon a time a man was told that he had an incurable illness. The news filled him with great sadness for he had dreamed dreams and hoped hopes, and now it seemed that they would never come true. One day he heard that there was a wizard who could do wonderful things for people, so he decided to visit him.

"What is it you want?" asked the wizard.

"I have dreamed dreams and hoped hopes," replied the man.

"What have you dreamed?"

"I have dreamed of a home, a home of my own to live in—a big home with many rooms and fine furniture."

"You have but to ask," said the wizard.

With that, he snapped his fingers and at once, in the twinkling of an eye, there stood a beautiful home. Nay, not a home, a palace—not even a palace, a castle. The castle was far bigger, far more beautiful than any he had ever dreamed of. There were almost too many rooms to count, and each one was filled with exquisite furniture. The man was filled with joy as he entered his house, walked its halls and explored its rooms.

But then, in time, he remembered the illness and again was filled with sadness. He returned to the wizard.

"What is it you want of me?" asked the wizard.

"I have dreamed dreams and I have hoped hopes," the man replied.

"What have you dreamed?"

"I have dreamed of food, food fit for a king. Food that would fill all my cravings, food as I have never eaten before."

"You have but to ask," said the wizard.

And he snapped his fingers. At once, in the twinkling of an eye, the castle table was covered with fine and delicious food. Never had the man seen such food or tasted such goodness. It was food fit for a hundred kings. He was filled with joy as he sat at the banquet table.

But then, in time, he remembered the sickness and the sadness came over him again. He returned to the wizard.

"What is it you want of me?" asked the wizard.

"I have dreamed dreams and I have hoped hopes," said the man.

"Tell me, what have you dreamed?"

"I have dreamed of clothes—fine, rich and beautiful clothes."

"You have but to ask," said the wizard.

Once again he snapped his fingers and at once the man was clothed in the finest clothes he had ever seen. His castle was filled with clothes, rich and beautiful clothes of the finest cloth imaginable. So the man walked his castle in his exquisite clothes, and sat at table to the finest of foods, and he was filled with happiness.

But then, in time, he remembered the incurable sickness, and a great sorrow overcame him.

"Why are you still sad?" asked the wizard. "Have I not fulfilled your dreams and hopes? Do you not have a castle, and clothes and food just as you wished? Why then are you still sad?"

"Because I have an incurable illness," the man cried.

"I can cure that," said the wizard.

The man's face quickly changed to hope.

"You can cure that!" he exclaimed. "Why, if you can cure that, what do I care about the rest? If you can cure the sickness, I don't care where I live, or what I eat or what I wear. None of that really matters if you can cure my sickness."

"You have but to ask," replied the wizard.

He then snapped his fingers, and in an instant, in the twinkling of an eye, the man was cured of his illness.

So the man walked away—away from the fine castle, away from the delicious foods, away from the exquisite clothes. He walked away from all of them—filled with joy, happier than he had ever been in his entire life.

What does this parable mean? Life is a terminal illness. When man first realized that life would come to an end, when he saw the grass die, and the leaves die, and the trees die, and animals die, and his companions die, and he knew that one day he, too, would die, he was filled with a great sadness.

One day he learned of a great wizard, a wonder worker—God. So man went before his God.

"What is it you want of me?" God asked.

"I have dreamed dreams and I have hoped hopes," replied man.

"Tell me, what is it you've dreamed?" asked the Lord God.

"I have dreamt of a house, a fine and luxurious house for me to live in," replied the man.

"You have but to ask," said God, and He snapped His fingers, and at once man had a place to live. A home of deep, rich earth with a mossy, green carpet, a home lit by the sun during the day, and the moon and the stars at night. And man made his home—homes of mud and mortar, homes of brick and stone, homes of wood and glass and steel, ranch homes and split levels, homes of one story and homes that reached into the sky.

The man in this parable was filled with joy over his home, and he walked its halls with great delight. But then, in time, he remembered he would die, and a great sadness overcame him. So he went back to God.

"What is it you want of me?" asked the Lord.

"Lord, I have dreamed dreams and hoped hopes!"

"Tell me what you have dreamed?"

"I've dreamed of food, food to fill my every yearning, food to satisfy my every hunger."

"You have but to ask," said the Lord God, and He snapped His fingers, and in an instant there was spread before the man a banquet of food, far beyond his dreams. Food from the earth was there: greens, vegetables and fruits of infinite variety. There was food from the seas—fish of every size and shape: lobster, crab, shrimps, scallops—pike, and trout and bass. Food from the land was there: beef, lamb, venison and pork. There was, in fact, every kind of meat. Food from the heavens was there: duck, geese, quail and pheasant. The man's banquet table was filled beyond his wildest imagining. So he ate and his heart was full of joy. But then, in time, he remembered he would die, and his sorrow returned. Again he went to his God.

"What is it you want of me?" asked God.

"I have dreamed dreams and hoped hopes," sighed the man.

"What have you dreamed?"

"I have dreamed of clothes—fine, rich and exquisite clothes. Clothes fit for a king!"

"You have but to ask," said the Lord, and again He snapped His fingers. In an instant, the man was clothed in magnificent attire. Cloth of wool, silk, velvet and cotton. Clothes of every size, shape, color and fabric. Warm clothes for winter and light clothes for summer. Clothes for morning, noon and night. Clothes fit for a hundred kings. So the man wore the clothes, and walked his castle, and ate his fill and in his heart, there was joy.

But then, once again, he remembered he must die. Again, a great sadness overwhelmed him.

"Why are you still sad?" asked God.

"Because I must die," the man cried.

"I can cure that," said God.

"You can cure that? You can cure death? Why, if you can cure death then I really don't care where I live, or what I eat or what I wear. None of that matters if you can cure death!"

"You have but to ask," said God.

With that, the Lord God snapped His fingers, and in an instant, in the twinkling of an infinite eye . . . *There Was Jesus!*

And the man walked away. Away from the castles of stone, and wood, and steel. Away from the food, and the exquisite clothes. The man walked away from all of them as if they were nothing. Cured of death, he walked away, his heart filled with joy—happier than in any dream he'd ever dreamt, happier than he'd ever hoped, happier than he had ever been in his entire life.

JOHNNY CRAB AND
THE LEPRECHAUN

I

Once upon a time, a long, long time ago—well, come to think of it—maybe it wasn't so long ago, in a place far, far away—well, come to think of it maybe it wasn't so far away either, there lived a young boy named Johnny. He wasn't a very pleasant boy. As a matter of fact he was quite a grouch. That's why everybody called him Johnny Crab.

One day Johnny Crab grabbed his bat and ball and set out for the park hoping to find some neighborhood kids for a baseball game. While on his way he ran into Sammy the Shrimp. Sammy was a short little fellow, hence the name, who was always excluded from everything because of his height. Johnny was in no mood to be bothered so he decided to just ignore him.

"Hi Johnny! Where are you going?" Johnny just continued walking. "Are you going to play baseball? Is that what you're going to do?"

"No. I'm going skiing," Johnny answered, unable to resist such an opening.

Undaunted by the retort Sammy continued, "Can I come too? Can I play?"

"No! Get lost." Johnny shot back.

"Please! I'll give you a quarter," he said reaching into his pocket.

"No!"

"I'll be your friend. I'll help you."

"How many times do I have to say no, Shrimp?"

"I know I'm small but I can be the bat boy. Let me be the bat boy."

"You bother me kid. Go away! If anybody saw a shrimp like you on our team, they'd laugh at us. Anyways, we've got more than enough kids so we don't need you."

"The other kids won't mind," Sammy pestered, "so can I? Please? Huh, can I?"

"Well, I mind and it's my bat and my ball and I say *no*!"

All during this conversation Johnny kept walking while Sammy circled around him and pulled on his sleeves jumping up and down with excitement. At this last refusal Sammy pulled so hard that he caused Johnny to fall down. This so infuriated him that he got up and chased Sammy the Shrimp away.

When he arrived at the park there were enough kids around to choose up sides and start a game. Johnny Crab's team was first up to bat.

The first batter up was Dodo Dennis. The way he stood at the plate was sufficient reason to explain why they called him Dodo. He stood there with his legs spread much too wide, the bat resting on his shoulder, mouth open, tongue hanging out to the side and a look of absolute nothing on his face. The ball whizzed past him. Dodo didn't budge. "Swing," yelled Johnny but it came much too late to help. "Strike one!" Again the ball was pitched right to him but Dodo stood motionless.

"Swing," shouted Johnny. "Swing, you Dodo." But it was already strike two. In sympathy the pitcher lobbed the ball over the plate making it excrutiatingly simple for the batter to hit. With all the breath he could muster from his lungs Johnny Crab screamed out "SWING." The ball flew past him. Dodo did nothing—absolutely nothing. "Strike three. You're out."

Johnny's temper could not be contained. He screamed and hollered at the batter, who just stood there unmoved. Johnny threw him out of the game.

The second batter didn't seem to offer much more hope. It was Silly Sally. She walked over to the plate holding the bat at the wrong end. When everyone saw her they doubled over and rolled in the grass laughing hysterically. Johnny walked over to her and demonstrated how to hold the bat but she insisted that it was much more comfortable her way and would not give in. This caused a great deal of commotion at home plate until the umpire shouted "Batter up." Johnny walked away in disgust throwing his arms up in the air. Silly Sally stood there holding the bat backwards.

Much to everyone's surprise Silly Sally swung and hit the very first pitch. It flew over the pitcher's head and bounced between third and second base rolling out toward left field. "Run" her teammates yelled, "run." Silly Sally dropped the bat and took off in a flash for third base. "No!" Johnny screamed, "the other way, the other way." Silly Sally arrived at third base and stood her ground. The left fielder picked up the ball and threw it to first base. "You're out," declared the umpire.

Johnny ranted as Silly Sally walked back. "Why did you run that way, stupid. You know you're supposed to go to first base. Why did you run to third, you ninny?"

"I'm left handed," she said indignantly. "Left handed people should be able to run that way."

Johnny was too upset to even attempt to answer such a stupid statement. So instead he threw her out of the game.

Alas, when Johnny saw who the third batter was, he slumped

down on the bench, elbows on his knees, face buried in his hands in disgust. It was Lightning Louie. Now if you think a name like Lightning Louie should, at this point, be cause for joy and not sorrow, let me correct you. Lightning Louie was a short, fat, pudgy faced, pudgy armed, pudgy fingered, pudgy legged boy. He was almost as wide as he was tall. Johnny Crab didn't even look up as Louie stood at bat.

He heard the kids shout, "Ball one!"

"Why does this have to happen to me?" Johnny groaned.

"Ball two!"

"Why can't I have normal friends?"

"Ball Three!"

"Oh, what's the use."

"Ball four!"

Lightning Louie's face lit up with joy, a grin across his pudgy face from ear to ear. He didn't have to swing. He probably wouldn't have hit the ball anyway. If he had, he would have had to run to first base. Now he could just take his time.

Louie carefully laid the bat on the ground and began strolling at a snail's pace toward first base. "Hurry up" they shouted but no one could rush Lightning Louie. Johnny Crab looked up in dismay. At that moment Louie saw a buttercup and stooped to pick it up.

"That's it," shouted Johnny. "That's it." He threw his hands up. "The game's over." He stormed over and retrieved his bat and ball. The others shouted at him to continue playing since they hadn't had a chance at bat yet. But Johnny wouldn't listen. He walked away to the jeers of his friends.

As he cut across to the other end of the park, he saw some boys from a different neighborhood fooling around. They were older than he and his friends but they looked a lot more normal. Johnny thought, I'll play ball with them and show the others what a real game of baseball is like.

Holding his bat in his left hand and tossing the ball up in the air and catching it with his right while trying to look as casual as possible, Johnny approached the strange group.

"Hey, you guys," his voice shaking a little bit, "would you like to play baseball?" The others stopped what they were doing and surrounded him suspiciously. "Sure kid," one of them said. He walked over and snatched the ball away from him. Someone else grabbed the bat and they all ran off laughing.

Johnny thought of chasing after them but they were bigger and he was afraid. Angry and frustrated he sat under a tree and began to cry.

II

He sat there for a while when a tiny voice suddenly shouted, "Get off me, you dim-witted knock-kneed dumbbell!"

He looked around but no one was there. "Who said that?" he asked, still looking.

"Me, you tow-headed excuse for a rag bag!"

Johnny could hear the voice clearly but could see no one. "Where are you?"

"Underneath you, you fat oaf! You're sitting on me." Johnny jumped up with a start and looked where he had been sitting. There was a rather large four-leaf clover near the tree he was resting against. Standing there right next to it, straightening himself out, was a leprechaun. In a flash, Johnny reached down and grabbed hold of him before he could get away. "Well, so you got me" snapped the leprechaun. "Now don't squeeze too hard or you'll ruffle me again. I suppose you'll be wanting a wish or somethin'?"

"Yes" said Johnny.

"Well, you can't have it because you didn't catch me fair and square. But I'll tell you what I will do. You like to play games, don't you?" Johnny didn't answer. All this was too much for him. He couldn't believe that this was really happening. "Well, I'll play some games with you like you've never played before. One for each leaf on the clover. Go ahead now, pluck one." So Johnny did.

GAME 1

Suddenly he was in a small room with a high—very high —ceiling. The room was totally empty except for an extremely tall chair that reached almost to the top of the room. Seated at the top of the chair was a very dignified looking man identified by the leprechaun as Mr. Harump. In front of Mr. Harump was a little door.

"The object of this game," said the leprechaun, "is to get out of the room. I will give you three hours to accomplish it. There is only one rule: don't knock over the chair. Now I'll be back in three hours." With that he vanished.

Johnny looked around the room to see if the leprechaun didn't have another secret way out. But there was none, just the one door near the ceiling. Johnny thought, "I will have to climb up the rungs of the chair like a ladder to get there." So he started to climb. At first it was easy. But the higher he got the farther apart the rungs were. When he approached the top, the last rung was too high for him to reach. He stretched as far as he could but he just couldn't reach it. Mr. Harump merely sat there eyeing him curiously.

At last Johnny saw he couldn't make it alone so he called to Mr. Harump for help. Mr. Harump sat with his arms folded, ignoring Johnny's pleas. "Be careful," Mr. Harump said, "Don't knock over the chair." Frustrated, Johnny tried to leap to the top rung but he didn't make it and went crashing down to the floor.

Once again he started up the chair only to arrive at the same impossible point. Again he asked Mr. Harump for help. If Mr. Harump would only grab his hand he could get up. But Mr. Harump paid no heed. He simply cautioned him again, "Don't knock over the chair." Another desperate attempt and down Johnny fell once more.

Furious, Johnny shouted up to him, "Help me up."

Mr. Harump glanced down his nose at the boy standing below him. "Don't you say please?"

"Please," shouted Johnny.

"No."

In frustration Johnny kicked the chair. Unmoved, Mr. Harump said, "Don't knock over the chair."

The time was passing quickly. "Maybe I can bribe him," Johnny thought. "Mr. Harump," he shouted, "I'll give you everything I have in my pockets if you help me up."

"No, and don't knock over the chair."

"I'll do anything you want only please help me."

"No, and don't knock over the chair." Johnny pleaded and begged but it was no use.

The leprechaun then appeared, "Well now, your time is almost up and I see you didn't make it."

"I have time for one last try," said Johnny and proceeded one final time up the chair. At the last rung he stretched desperately while Mr. Harump, arms folded, just looked down his nose at him. Again he leaped and again he missed falling all the way down to where the leprechaun stood laughing. The fall this time was so violent that the chair was rocking dangerously.

Mr. Harump shouted down, "Don't knock over the chair," just as the leprechaun announced that the time was up.

Johnny was so furious that he lifted his foot and kicked the chair with all his might. The chair toppled and down came Mr. Harump. The leprechaun roared with laughter as he said to Johnny, "You lose! As a matter of fact, you both lose! Pluck the next leaf," and he handed Johnny the clover.

GAME 2

Johnny found himself in a large open courtyard empty of everything except for a solitary chair placed right in the middle.

"This is a simple enough game," the leprechaun said. "You must sit in this chair absolutely still for six hours. You may not budge, or move a muscle or twitch an eye—nothing."

"What's the purpose of this game?" Johnny asked.

"There's one thing you can do," he answered. "Only one thing and if you do it right you will win the game."

"What's that?"

"You can say the word 'yes,' but only once. And you must say it to the right person or you lose. Remember, you have six hours." Having said that the leprechaun vanished.

Johnny sat down in the chair, settled into a comfortable position and waited. Shortly, some people began entering the courtyard. Because Johnny was seated by himself in the very center staring blankly ahead, he drew everyone's attention. They looked at him curiously. At first they wondered if he were real. They tried talking to him but to no avail. He in no way responded to them, neither by word nor gesture.

Then the people began to make a game of it. One after another they came before him, making faces and gesturing, trying frantically to get a response. But Johnny sat there immobile, scrutinizing each

47

participant, wondering who was the right person to respond to. "There's plenty of time," he thought, "no need to rush. I must be sure to respond to the right one."

One hour passed. Then another and another and another. The procession of people in the courtyard continued. Still Johnny sat there not moving a muscle.

The fifth hour had just begun when the leprechaun appeared. "That's it," he said, "I've had enough of this game. I don't like it any more."

"But it's not time yet," Johnny cried out.

"I don't care," he answered with the toss of a hand. "The game's over and you lose. Now pluck the next leaf."

GAME 3

Johnny and the leprechaun were now standing at the edge of a very dense forest. Rather irritated over the last contest and tiring of the entire situation, Johnny expressed his annoyance in the way he said, "Now what?"

"This game is much more interesting," smiled the leprechaun. "All you have to do is make your way through the forest in nine hours and you win. I'll even make it easy for you. You can ask anyone you want for help." With that he disappeared. Only the echo of his laughter lingered behind. This test was more to Johnny's liking. He had often thought of himself as some kind of early American frontiersman like Daniel Boone, carving his way through uncharted wild lands. For a moment he wished he had his compass with him but then, remembering that he didn't know where he was, he decided it wouldn't have made any difference. With his chest out and his head high he marched into the woods like a soldier.

He simply followed the path before him. It circled and snaked through the forest and ended in a fork. Johnny traveled to the right. He followed that path until it too came to a fork. This time he opted for the left. That path broke into several more before Johnny decided that he was lost.

Just at that moment he saw a group of people gathering wood. He approached them bravely. "Can you help me through the forest?" he asked, remembering that it was fair to get help.

"No," they said rather happily, "just follow us."

"Then you mean *yes*, don't you?" Johnny asked.

One of them came forward and said, "If we said *yes* then we wouldn't show you, would we? But we did say *no* so follow us."

"This is confusing," Johnny thought, but rather than discuss the point he tagged along behind them.

When they came to a fork in the road, the leader shouted to the others, "Here we have to go right." Then, without the slightest hesitation he proceeded down the path to the left.

Johnny ran up to him, "I thought you said we should go right?"

"I did," he answered.

"Then why are you going left?"

He looked at Johnny as if he were some sort of confused child. "Left," he said, "is that way," pointing to the right. "And right," he said, "is that way," pointing to the left. "We must go right," he repeated and continued down the left path.

Johnny was more confused now but followed along obediently. Soon the path ended and they were walking through thick brush. Afraid that he would lose the others who walked ahead much more assuredly than he, Johnny cried out to the leader, "Please hold my hand so that I don't lose you."

"If I did that, I wouldn't be able to walk."

"Why not?" Johnny was beginning to get annoyed.

"How do you expect me to walk with one hand?" he said as he lifted one foot and pointed to the other.

"That's your foot," Johnny said. "I don't want to hold your foot. I want to hold your hand." Then Johnny extended his right hand toward the leader.

"That's not your hand," the leader snapped. "That's your foot!"

Johnny was angry now. "That's not my foot, that's my hand."

"It is not," the leader shot back. "This is your hand," he said, indignantly pointing to his foot. "And THIS is your foot," gesturing forcefully at his hand. "Tell him!" the leader said to the others.

"That's wrong," they replied, smiling at the leader who smiled approvingly back at them.

"That's what I said," Johnny said to the leader, "They are agreeing with me."

"We are agreeing with our leader," they said huffily.

"Wait a minute," Johnny said. "Which way is left?" They all pointed to the right. "No," he shouted.

"Well that's what we all say, No! So why are you arguing with us?" they scolded.

"But you mean *yes* when you say *no*," he cried.

"We don't understand you," they retorted. When we say *yes* we mean *yes* and when we say *no* we mean *no*. What are you talking about?"

"Listen"—Johnny was now exasperated—"just answer *yes* or *no*." He pointed to the left and said, "Is that left?"

"Yes," they all responded.

"Then let's all go left," Johnny said. At this point the entire group started walking to the right. "No," he cried, "you're going to the right."

"Yes," they said, "right's that way," and they pointed to the left.

At this point Johnny became so confused he didn't know which way to go. The leprechaun appeared. "I see you didn't make it. Well, time's up and you lose again." He stood there grinning from ear to ear. He crossed one leg over the other flippantly and held out the clover with just one leaf left. "Pluck the last leaf!" he ordered.

GAME 4

They were standing in an open field. In the center of the field was a table. Resting on the table was the most beautiful trophy Johnny had ever seen.

"Do you like it?" asked the leprechaun.

"Yes. Very much!" Johnny answered.

"Well, maybe you'll win it. You have to qualify. Let me see how fast you can run." Johnny ran around the field at breakneck speed. "Wonderful," the leprechaun shouted. That was the first time he had said anything pleasant to the boy. "For that I will give you a medal." He placed a rather large iron medal hanging from a heavy chain around Johnny's neck.

"Now let me see how far you can run," he said. Johnny ran around the field over and over until he almost fell over with exhaustion. Twenty-five times he circled the field. "Wonderful," said the leprechaun, jumping with joy. Johnny was winded but pleased. "For that I will give you another medal." He then placed an even larger medal around Johnny's neck.

"Now let me see how long you can hop on one foot." Johnny did as he was asked and managed to hop for quite a long time. Again he won a medal.

Johnny was pleased with this contest. He felt certain that the leprechaun was pleased too and would give him the trophy. He stood before the table, three medals hanging from his neck, panting heavily but happy.

"Now do I get the trophy?" he gasped.

"Not quite. Let's see how well you do hopping on the other foot?"

Again Johnny began to hop. The jangling medals weighed him down. This time he didn't hop half as long as the last time. None the less the leprechaun was pleased with his performance and awarded him still another medal.

"Now do I get the trophy?" he panted.

"Not quite," said the smiling leprechaun, "there's one last test before our time is up. You must race me around the field and the winner gets the trophy." Before Johnny could utter a word of protest the leprechaun took off with a bound. Johnny tried desperately to catch up to him but it was no use. He was much too tired and worn out from the other things he had done. While he ran, the heavy medals weighed him down mercilessly till he could barely move. The leprechaun won easily. "Well, you lost again," he stated rather matter-of-factly. "You lost all four games." Then he began laughing. He was laughing uncontrollably as he began to fade away. "You lost, you lost," he was saying, "but then again maybe you didn't. Just maybe, you didn't."

When the leprechaun disappeared, Johnny sat down against a tree to rest. Later, when he got up, he realized he was holding in his hand the stem of what was once a four-leaf clover. He started walking back home through the park when he came upon his bat and ball where the others had thrown them having tired of their game. He picked them up still thinking of his encounter with the mischievous imp.

From out of nowhere Sammy the Shrimp hurled himself at

Johnny. "Are you going to play ball, Johnny?" Johnny paid no attention to him. He just kept walking, thinking about what the leprechaun had said. Sammy persisted in his usual way, circling around Johnny, jumping up and down, pulling on his sleeve.

Annoyed at this distraction he turned on Sammy and shouted, "Don't knock me over!" Suddenly Johnny stopped. "Don't knock me over. . . ." He almost whispered it this time—remembering.

He looked down at Sammy. "Yes Sammy," he said. "Sure you can play. As a matter of fact we're all going to play. You, me, Dodo Dennis, Silly Sally, Lightning Louie. Everybody. We're all going to play the best baseball game we ever played."

"That's wonderful," Sammy shouted. "That's great. But how come you changed your mind?"

"Well, Sammy" Johnny said, parroting the leprechaun. "I just spent the whole afternoon playing a game. And you know something," he said seriously, "I think I won!"

THE PEASANT AND
THE PRINCESS

"The Kingdom of Heaven is like this. Once there was a man who went out early in the morning to hire some men to work in his vineyard. He agreed to pay them the regular wage, a silver coin a day, and sent them to work in his vineyard. He went out again to the market place at nine o'clock and saw some men standing there doing nothing, so he told them, 'You also go and work in the vineyard, and I will pay you a fair wage.' So they went. Then at twelve o'clock and again at three o'clock he did the same thing. It was nearly five o'clock when he went to the market place and saw some other men still standing there. 'Why are you wasting the whole day here doing nothing?' he asked them. 'No one hired us,' they answered. 'Well, then, you go and work in the vineyard,' he told them.

"When evening came, the owner told his foreman, 'Call the workers and pay them their wages, starting with those who were hired last." The men who had begun to work at five o'clock were paid a silver coin each. So when the men who were the first to be hired came to be paid, they thought they would get more; but they too were given a silver coin each. They took their money and started grumbling against the employer. 'These men who were hired last worked only one hour,' they said, 'while we put up with a whole day's work in the hot sun—yet you paid them the same as you paid us!' 'Listen, friend,' the owner answered one of them, 'I have not cheated you. After all, you agreed to do a day's work for one silver coin. Now take your pay and go home. I want to give this man who was hired last as much as I gave you. Don't I have the right to do as I wish with my own money? Or are you jealous because I am generous?' "

And Jesus concluded, "So those who are last will be first, and those who are first will be last" (Matthew 20:1-16).

Then Peter came to Jesus and asked, "Lord, if my brother keeps on sinning against me, how many times do I have to forgive him? Seven times?"

"No, not seven times," answered Jesus, "but seventy times seven, because the Kingdom of Heaven is like this. Once there was a king who decided to check on his servants' accounts. He had just begun to do so when one of them was brought in who owed him millions of dollars. The servant did not have enough to pay his debt, so the king ordered him to be sold as a slave, with his wife and his children and all that he had, in order to pay the debt. The servant fell on his knees before the king. 'Be patient with me,' he begged, 'and I will pay you everything!' The king felt sorry for him, so he forgave him the debt and let him go.

"Then the man went out and met one of his fellow servants who owed him a few dollars. He grabbed him and started choking him.

'Pay back what you owe me!' he said. His fellow servant fell down and begged him, 'Be patient with me, and I will pay you back!' But he refused; instead, he had him thrown into jail until he should pay the debt. When the other servants saw what had happened, they were very upset and went to the king and told him everything. So he called the servant in. 'You worthless slave!' he said. 'I forgave you the whole amount you owed me, just because you asked me to. You should have had mercy on your fellow servant, just as I had mercy on you.' The king was very angry, and he sent the servant to jail to be punished until he should pay back the whole amount."

And Jesus concluded, "That is how my Father in heaven will treat every one of you unless you forgive your brother from your heart" (Matthew 18:21-25).

I

Once upon a time, a long, long time ago in a castle very near the end of the earth there lived a great and mighty king. His castle was the talk of the whole world. Few people had ever seen it but those who did told wonderful stories about it. It was bigger and more beautiful than any castle anyone had ever looked upon. Its towers were made of gold, the walls were of silver and the doors were all of bronze. All the rooms and halls shone with a brilliance brighter than the sun for they were lit not by candles or torches but by diamonds which sparkled everywhere.

Even the people who lived in the castle were exceptional. They were the tallest, the strongest, the most handsome, the most beautiful, the most talented people, who came there from all over the world. Each year the king would hold a contest to determine who should come to live in the castle. Only the most gifted would compete and only the best of those were chosen to enter. So it was that all over the earth people prepared themselves for the annual event. For endless hours they worked: jugglers juggled, dancers danced, acrobats tumbled, wise men studied, strong men exercised and runners ran.

As the great day drew near, people from everywhere, contestants and spectators, began their journey to the great field where the events would take place. Slowly the area began to fill. There were people everywhere. Some were laughing and celebrating while others still prepared furiously for the upcoming contests. The air was electric with excitement and anticipation.

The king's messenger sounded the trumpet call. "Let the games begin," he cried. The crowds settled to a hush. The king was seated in his throne. The contestants came forward. With a respectful bow to their lord they began. Never had the world witnessed such great displays of talent—music, art, dance, literature—talents of every conceivable kind in endless succession.

When each group had finished performing their specialty, the people themselves would acclaim whom the best performer was, and that person would solemnly take his place at the side of the king. So the events proceeded: the performers putting forth their best—the crowd acclaiming the winners.

At last came the final contest, the test of strength. Seven huge stones were placed at one end of the field. The contestants stepped forward in turn before the king where each bowed in respect. Huge muscles, strong backs and thick legs glistened in the sunlight. The crowd watched in awesome silence as these great behemoths came forward one at a time. Suddenly there was a commotion. The spectators looked around to find out the cause. The noise grew louder until it broke forth in thunderous laughter. Out of the crowd and into the open courtyard stepped a bedraggled peasant. As he took his place beside the other contestants the people laughed hysterically. The contrast between the peasant and the strong men was incredibly ridiculous. Where they were tall, he was uncommonly short; where they were muscular, he was thin and puny; where they were dressed in elegant gymnastic clothes, he was dressed in rags.

But the mood of the crowd was quick to change. From shouts of merriment and laughter, they moved to annoyance, then impatience and finally anger. "Take the peasant away," they shouted. "He is an insult to the others," they cried. "Remove him, remove him." Others began to take up the chant. "REMOVE HIM."

Unperturbed by the heckling crowd, the king's messenger stood and sounded the horn. "Let all who have come to compete, compete," he announced.

The crowd fell into a sullen silence. "Let it be," someone said. "The fool will not be able to match himself against the others."

Again the messenger spoke, this time to the contestants. "Carry the stones from one end of the field to the other."

Thus the contest began. The huge stones were a formidable test of the men's strength. One by one they came forward and, by lifting or pushing or pulling, they set about the task. After a time some withdrew because it was too much for them. Some others continued, completing the feat. The crowd cheered and applauded them. Teams of horses would then drag the stones back and the next group would try. So it proceeded for hours. The peasant sat on the ground, waiting, doing nothing.

At last when all the others had finished only the peasant remained. Once again the crowd began to laugh and jeer. Unmoved, the peasant rose and walked over to the last remaining stone. He stood there quietly, just staring intently at it. Now the whole crowd took up the sport of heckling the peasant.

"Look well at it," someone shouted. "See what it is that will break your back."

"It's bigger than you, little man."

"And cleaner," someone added to the growing delight of the crowd.

"Take a mighty breath and try blowing it away." More laughter and still more followed while the peasant stooped over the rock examining it ever so closely.

When his examination was finally done, he stood erect and reached into his peasant robe. The crowd became curious and silent. From beneath his tunic, the peasant took out a mallet. Once again he examined the rock, this time with his hand, running it lightly over the face of it—feeling it as if searching for something. He then took the mallet and with three quick hammer blows, the rock shattered. He bent over, picked up a piece of stone and proceeded slowly to the other end of the field. The spectators watched in disbelieving silence. The peasant returned to fetch another piece of stone and carry it to the other end of the field.

As the crowd realized what he was doing they started shouting their disapproval. "That is unfair."

"He is not strong like the others."

"He is a fool. Take him away."

"He did not work to build himself up as the others did. He did not even practice. Do not let him finish. Stop him."

But the peasant continued until the entire stone lay at the other end of the field. "No," they shouted. "No," in endless chant.

The king rose. The peasant waited to be called to his side. The king raised his arms to silence the throng.

"What have you to say of this man?" asked the king to those contestants who now stood at his side.

"NO!" they called as the crowd had done. "He must not be allowed to win. He did not work nor struggle as we did. It would discourage others from trying."

"What have you to say to these claims?" the king asked the peasant.

Looking solemn and somehow wise the peasant answered, "Your majesty, would you have your servants bring before you a fat man and a thin one?"

"Do as he says," commanded the king to the surprise and dismay of the crowd. The two men were selected and brought before the king. "What would you have them do?" he asked.

Calmly, resolutely, the peasant said, "Place before them two meals, each identical to the other in every way including the amount." The servants did as they were told. The peasant then said to the two, "Eat until you can eat no more."

So the two men began eating their meals while the king, the victors, the peasant and the crowd watched silently.

The thin man finished first having eaten less than half of what was placed before him. "I am done. I can eat no more," he said and sat back. The fat man continued to eat until almost all of his meal was finished. "I now am full," he said, "and can eat no more."

The peasant walked over to the thin man. "Would you eat what the fat man has not finished?"

"I cannot," he replied. "I am full."

He then went to the fat man. "Would you eat what the thin man has not finished?"

"I cannot," he replied, "I too am full."

The peasant stood before the King. "Does the thin man begrudge the fat man because he has eaten more or is the thin man satisfied since he has eaten his full? Does the fat man begrudge the thin man because he, the fat man, cannot eat what was left over or is he satisfied now that he has eaten and is full?"

The king was pleased with the peasant's wisdom. The crowd could not or would not comprehend it. How could one so poor and shabby ever speak wisdom? How could one so ragged dare to enter the king's court? They would not hail him as victor. They dared not.

The king rose before the assembled throng to give his judgment. "Join me at my side," he beckoned to the peasant. "Take your place with the victors." The trumpets blaring signaled that the contests were over. The king and the victors rode off to the castle and the crowd returned home to the four corners of the earth.

II

To celebrate the completion of the games and to welcome the new victors to the kingdom, the king held a ball in the great hall of the palace. The men were dressed in fine robes and the women in rich and beautiful gowns. It was a picture of elegance and splendor. Only the peasant was dressed as before in ragged clothes and tattered shoes, a pitiful contrast to the beauty of the occasion. There was great merriment, feasting and dancing but he sat quietly at table observing the others.

When the king's daughter entered the hall all attention and activity were instantly directed at her. She was beautiful beyond description. She seemed more radiant than the diamonds that lit the room. The king summoned the newest members of his court, introduced them to the princess and gave to each of them the great honor of dancing with his daughter.

The orchestra began playing again while one by one they danced with her. She waltzed with the grace of a swan around and around the great hall. At last, when all the others had had a turn, the peasant came forward. The courtiers and ladies were embarrassed by his presence, trying not to look at him as he approached the princess. She stood there, a vision of loveliness, all dressed in white while he looked like some sort of foolish troll bowing before her, taking her hand. The orchestra began to play and as he turned to take her in his arms he clumsily stepped on one of her shoes. It was to be expected. What else could one so obviously ill-bred be expected to do. The princess cried out in pain and anger.

"You stepped on me," she shrieked drawing everyone's attention. "You clumsy fool. See what you've done. You've stepped on my shoe and you've made it dirty like you. I will have to leave the party now all because of you."

The peasant was embarrassed by what had happened. He was ashamed and sorry for causing the princess such distress.

"Forgive me. I am sorry," he stammered.

"Forgive you? How can I forgive you? I will have to leave the ball. I can't dance with a dirty shoe." She turned around for the others to see her plight. They quickly came to comfort her.

The peasant struggled to make amends. "Please forgive me," he repeated. "If only there were something I could do."

The princess turned and shouted to him, "If you want me to forgive you then quick, bring me a new pair of shoes." At once the peasant left the hall. Minutes later he returned holding in his hands a beautiful pair of golden glass slippers. The princess, surrounded by her ladies-in-waiting, stopped her sobbing to see what manner of shoes a lowly peasant would bring to her. She was surprised and pleased when she saw them but was careful not to show it. "They will have to do," she said and snatched them away from him. The peasant withdrew to his lonely seat at table.

The ball continued but the peasant did not dare again to approach the princess. Indeed he sat by himself for the entire evening. When the tower clock struck the hour of midnight the party ended. All the revelers went off to their rooms for the night.

When the princess arrived in her bedchamber she felt a strange uneasiness about the evening's activities. True, she had danced with all the victors as she had in previous years and they were as pleasant and pleasing to her now as the ones in the past, but still she had not found one whom she might desire to marry. There were many handsome men at the ball but certainly none that could match her beauty. Nor could those who were wise or talented, she thought, match her wisdom and grace. It was to be another fruitless year of waiting until the next new group of winners would arrive. She heaved a sigh of annoyance as she bent over to remove her shoes.

At first she thought her feet had swollen from the long night of dancing because the glass slippers would not come off. She tugged and pulled at one and then the other but they stuck to her feet. What little patience she had vanished as she tumbled to the floor wrestling with the shoes. Exasperated, she called in her servants to help but none of them could remove the slippers. They held hard and fast.

"What nonsense is this?" she screamed out. "That awful peasant has done this to me. Bring him here immediately." At once the peasant was summoned and brought to her chamber.

"These slippers will not come off," she chided. "What have you done to me?"

"Forgive me, my princess," he whispered.

" 'Forgive me, forgive me.' Is that all you can say? Well, I won't forgive you unless you remove these awful slippers from my feet."

"I shall immediately," he said. He knelt down and without the slightest effort took the golden glass slippers off.

The ease with which he did it surprised the princess. "Who are you and how is it you came to be here?"

"Like the others, I competed and won."

"You are not like the others," the princess shot back quickly. "You are not at all like any of the others. Why would you possibly want to come here?"

"I have come here to marry you," was his simple reply.

His answer at first left the princess speechless. If it weren't so foolish, she would have been angry. Instead, she laughed. The idea was so ridiculous that she laughed even harder.

"Marry me. Why you are not only ugly, you are a fool. Be off and consider yourself fortunate that I don't have you thrown into the dungeon for all the distress you've caused me. Now go, I don't want to see you again—ever." Without a word the peasant left her chamber.

What happened afterwards did not happen quickly, but became only gradually noticeable over the following weeks and months. The princess began to grow ugly. First the beautiful white glow of her skin began to fade. It became dull and yellowish like tarnish. Then her hair lost its lustre. Wrinkles began to appear on her face and hands which grew deeper like scars over the passing days. The people of the court saw the changes happening to the princess but were careful not to mention them. They did not want to offend her and they also remembered her quick temper. Instead they tried to talk of things that would make her laugh. The only thing she found amusing though, was to retell the story of the ugly peasant who had wanted to marry her. This would cause her to break into fits of laughter. "Imagine me marrying that creature. Why, he even smelled," she said as she put her fingers to her nose. The others imitated her and claimed that they could almost smell him from there. Indeed they'd noticed a real trace of a peculiar peasant odor in the room. Even as they laughed it grew stronger. He must be hiding in the room they thought, so they made a game of looking for him. They searched behind the drapes and in the closets and even in drawers to the great amusement of the princess.

In the days and weeks that followed, the princess noticed the smell everywhere. It grew stronger and stronger and seemed to follow her wherever she went. The others were aware of it too but were careful not to mention it anymore. Instead they tried to amuse the princess by telling her funny stories about happenings around the castle. When these failed to amuse her they asked her to tell them about the ugly, smelly peasant again. This she would do with great delight, each time adding some new observation that would set everyone laughing.

One time she said, "Not only was he ugly and smelly but his ragged clothes were horrid. They hung on him like floppy pantaloons on a scarecrow." The new description delighted her listeners at the time, who began to strike different poses imitating scarecrows. Indeed, they would have all lingered about in their merriment for the rest of the day but for the awful smell in the room. In appropriate haste they made their exits leaving the princess to laugh alone.

As the end of the year approached there was again much excitement about the coming contests. The castle was decorated for the victory ball. The food for the banquet was prepared. The courtiers and ladies set out their finest clothes. The princess spent the last month in seclusion so that her grand entrance would have added importance.

At last the great day arrived and with much fanfare the victors were escorted to the castle by the king. That evening the great hall was once again filled with music and merriment. Shortly after the dancing had begun, when the proper amount of time had lapsed, a trumpet sounded to announce the arrival of the princess. All eyes turned to the staircase. Then the princess made her appearance.

There was an audible gasp from the assembled crowd. There at the head of the stairs was not the beautiful princess of years past. Instead there stood an ugly, pale wisp of a woman who looked more old than young. Even the beautiful gown she wore hung heavily on her frail body giving her the appearance of a dressed up scarecrow. As she slowly descended the stairs, a distinctly unpleasant odor accompanied her.

No one moved. Indeed, no one even uttered a word so great was their surprise. The entire assembly stood frozen like statues. Even when the princess reached the bottom stair and stumbled on her own gown not one person hastened to her. She lay there on the floor, sobbing.

At long last someone came forward through the gaping crowd to where the princess fell. He bent over to take her hand. When the princess reached up to take it, she looked into the face of the most handsome man she had ever seen. She was overwhelmed by his beauty and his graciousness. She rose to her feet embarrassed at her clumsiness.

"May I have this dance?" he asked.

She could not answer. He took her in his arms and the orchestra began to play. The others continued to stand dumbstruck while the couple started to dance. No sooner had she begun to dance with him when she turned and stepped on his foot. She had never done that before, not in her whole life. Her face flushed with embarrassment.

"Forgive me," she apologized for the first time in her life.

"Gladly," he said instantly, "think nothing of it."

It was too much for her, her pitiful condition and his kindness. She ran off sobbing into the garden. The handsome young man ran out after her.

"What's wrong?" he asked.

"I am so wretched," she cried. "Why don't you leave me and join the others."

"But I came for you," he replied.

"For me?" She was startled out of her tears.

"For me?" she repeated. "But why?"

"I came here to marry you."

"Alas," she thought, "after waiting all these years for the right person." Then she cried out, "How could you possibly want to marry me?"

"But princess, why should I not want to marry you?"

"Because I am no longer beautiful but ugly."

"That makes no difference to me."

"Because I smell," she added.

"Nor does that matter."

"Because I look like a scarecrow," she pleaded.

"No matter."

"But how can you want me? I am a terrible princess not even worthy enough to marry a peasant."

"My princess," he said softly, "I am that peasant."

Before she could utter another word he took her in his arms and kissed her. At once she became the beautiful young princess again. Hand in hand they walked back into the great hall and danced into forever.

THE YELLOW MAN

"At that time the Kingdom of Heaven will be like this. Once there were ten girls who took their oil lamps and went out to meet the bridegroom. Five of them were foolish, and the other five were wise. The foolish ones took their lamps but did not take any extra oil with them, while the wise ones took containers full of oil for their lamps. The bridegroom was late in coming, so the girls began to nod and fall asleep.

"It was already midnight when the cry rang out, 'Here is the bridegroom! Come and meet him!' The ten girls woke up and trimmed their lamps. Then the foolish ones said to the wise ones, 'Let us have some of your oil, because our lamps are going out.' 'No, indeed,' the wise ones answered, 'there is not enough for you and for us. Go to the store and buy some for yourselves.' So the foolish girls went off to buy some oil; and while they were gone, the bridegroom arrived. The five girls who were ready went in with him to the wedding feast, and the door was closed.

"Later the other girls arrived. 'Sir, sir! Let us in!' they cried out. 'Certainly not! I don't know you,! the bridegroom answered."

And Jesus concluded, "Watch out, then, because you do not know the day or the hour" (Matthew 25:1-13).

I

Once upon a time, not so long ago there was a little village in a valley where the land was rocky and hard and the farmers struggled to grow their crops. The children had little time to play because there was too much work to be done. Young and old had to work to stay alive.

Sunday was the only day of rest. After church services, all the village people gathered in the square where the adults would sit and gossip and the children would play in the grass. More often than not the talk was about how difficult life in the valley was and that doubtless, the wicked witch of the frightful forest was the cause of it all.

"Be careful how you talk," said Mrs. Crowe as she gave a quick glance over her left shoulder toward the forest. "They say she has a way of hearing everything."

"What does it matter?" said young Mrs. Miller. "Life is already difficult in this valley. Even the old witch would find it difficult to make things harder. What we should all do is pack up and leave —lock, stock, and barrel. Then she can spook herself." The thought of what she had just said made her laugh. The others thought the idea was funny too and they broke into hysterical laughter.

Old Mrs. Cotter sat there knitting quietly. Without so much as looking up from her needles she said in a calm, matter-of-fact tone, "Where would you go?"

"Indeed," repeated Mrs. Crowe, who did not join in the laughter of the younger women. "Where would you go?"

The laughter stopped abruptly. Joy, like all other things in the valley, was short-lived.

"Surely there must be a place; there's got to be more than this," came an exasperated reply.

"Indeed," snorted Mrs. Crowe, indignant over the frivolousness of the younger women. "There's nothing but high mountains on one side and the frightful forest on the other. You girls would do well to take things more seriously."

Certainly it was a hopeless situation they thought as they glanced over their left shoulders at the frightful forest. It was the domain of the wicked witch and no one dared look straight at it, let alone venture into it. The mountains on the other side were so high that they were always covered with snow from halfway to the top. Life in the valley was difficult, but not impossible. To get out of the valley seemed impossible, not difficult.

As they looked silently at the mountains they noticed a peculiar, yellow object moving downward.

"Look," shouted the children who noticed it at the same time. Even the men stopped their serious conversation to glance at the mountains.

The peculiar, yellow object neither fell downwards nor flew downwards, but seemed to drift in that direction. Now, all the villagers were viewing the phenomenon with rapt attention.

When whatever-it-was reached the bottom, all the villagers hastened over to see it. What they saw astounded them. It was a man, a stranger. They had never seen a stranger in the village. He looked like any other man except he was dressed all in yellow. He wore yellow shoes and yellow pants plus a yellow jacket with a yellow vest underneath. His shirt and tie were yellow. Even his hair was a golden yellow. He was yellow all over right down to the gold ring on his finger.

One of the men in the crowd, the mayor, who felt it was his duty to speak for the people on such an occasion, although he never had to do so before, since nothing like this had ever happened before, who was obviously frightened by the peculiar stranger because he was shaking terribly, remembering that someone once told him years back that you shouldn't talk to strangers, which was rather odd because there never were any, ended up doing absolutely nothing but scratching his head.

It was Mrs. Cotter, while she was still knitting, who broke the silence. "Where are you from?" she asked.

"The sun," he replied and broke into a hearty laugh.

"Why did you come here?" she questioned, unsmiling, never dropping a stitch.

"I didn't," he answered. "That is, I didn't come to be here but to go through here. I am on my way to somewhere else."

"Somewhere else," cried one of the women. "I knew there was somewhere else."

"Hush now," reprimanded Mrs. Crowe. "Indeed," she said to the yellow man. "Somewhere else. There is no place else."

"But there is," said the yellow man, "and I am on my way there."

Not caring what Mrs. Crowe might say, young Mrs. Miller pushed her way forward and asked, "Where is it?"

"Just beyond the forest," he said pointing and looking straight at it. There was a gasp from the crowd. No one had ever looked directly at the frightful forest. They had always looked at it over their left shoulders. If they had to point in that direction, they'd have to use their left hand and bend their finger so as not to point directly at it.

"Indeed. No one has ever gone through the forest. The wicked witch lives there. She'd never let anyone pass through."

"Oh, I'll admit it won't be easy, but I have just the thing that will help me."

"What's that?" cried Mrs. Miller hopefully.

The yellow man reached into his pocket and pulled out a yellow seed. It looked very much like a kernel of corn.

"What are you going to do with that?" one of the children asked.

"Plant it. Wait for the fruit to grow, then take that with me as food for the journey through the forest."

The thought of leaving the village was too much for Mrs. Miller and the other young women.

"May we go too? May all of us go with you?" they cried.

"Most certainly if you want to. I have enough seeds for all of you. One for each person who wishes to go," he said as he pulled out a handful of seeds.

At last the mayor found his voice. "We must discuss this. Let us all gather in the square."

The excitement and commotion were something they had never seen before in the village. Everyone was called and everyone came.

There were so many people that they couldn't all fit in the square. So, with much hubub and ado, they went to a little hill at the edge of the village. The Mayor and the yellow man stood at the top while the villagers sat in groups on the grass around them.

The Mayor briefly told everyone about the yellow stranger because he was certain that not everyone was there when they saw him arrive and he wanted to be sure that everyone knew what it was all about, that is, what the stranger had told them although it probably wasn't necessary since everyone was talking about it so they must all know about it anyways.

One of the ladies interrupted the Mayor and asked the yellow man about the place he was going to. "What is it like?"

He painted a picture which to these hard beset people seemed like nothing less than paradise. A beautiful land with happy people.

"About the seed," a farmer asked. "What are we supposed to do with it? What's it for?"

Here the yellow man took great pains to explain. "You must plant the seed and tend it carefully. Make sure that it has enough water. Be careful not to let the weeds choke it. Then, above all, you must wait for it to come to fruit."

"How will we know when it is ready?"

"I will be here with you. Then we will gather the fruit and start on our journey. Each person will be given one seed. Each one must see to his own plant. No one can take any fruit other than what he has grown himself. This is how it must be."

There was much commotion about this with much explaining and repeating. Then Mrs. Cotter said, "What if we don't care to go?"

"I will give every person a seed. What he chooses to do with it is up to him," he replied to her and also the crowd.

"How will we make it through the frightful forest?" a timid voice inquired.

"Yes, what about the wicked witch?"

The thought of the witch kindled a chorus of questions from the crowd.

"The food will give you strength. You need not be afraid. She will do you no harm."

"Indeed," chimed in Mrs. Crowe. "No harm, indeed. What proof do you have?"

"You have my word," said the yellow man who, without another utterance, passed through the crowd giving each one a seed.

Some of the villagers joined with Mrs. Cotter and Mrs. Crowe and threw their seeds away.

"Stuff and nonsense. Here we know what we have, as bad as that may seem. But there," said Mrs. Crowe looking over her left shoulder and pointing with a crooked finger of her left hand, "that way is foolishness."

The meeting ended as the golden sun set behind the hill where the villagers were gathered.

Meanwhile, in the frightful forest, in a tree hut built at the top of one of the highest trees, the wicked witch watched closely over all that was happening. Nestled in the crook of her arm, a black cat purred as she stroked its fur and listened closely to all that was said.

"Plant the seeds, ehh?" she cackled. "We shall see. We shall see."

II

As the first rays of morning filled the valley all the people busied themselves with their daily tasks. Only this day, many of them added a new chore, the planting of the golden seed. With great care each one cleared a little plot of soil, removed all weeds, raked the difficult ground, implanted the seed, watered it and waited for it to grow. Each one planted his own seed and tended to his own plant as the yellow man had instructed them. The new chore became part of the daily ritual, so that soon new plants began to sprout throughout the valley.

It was about then that the wicked witch began to stir up a special brew in her cauldron. With each ingredient she added to the boiling, smoking pot, she shrieked with evil delight. When the work was done, when the last tongue of dried-out toad slid between the bubbles, she danced in wild frenzy around the hut. In the corner, the cat meowed knowingly.

"Well, Lucifer, my pet, it is ready. We shall see now how well their precious little plants will grow. Golden man or not, they will not leave my valley. . . . NEVER!"

With that she dipped her ladle into the foul brew and drank until she had finished it all. She walked to the window that overlooked the valley, stood there with her arms outstretched as if to encompass all of it, then let out a long silent scream. From deep within her a fierce, hot breath welled up and flowed out of her mouth gaining momentum as it passed over the forest covering the valley with concentrated, dry heat. On and on it came, never losing its force, always growing in intensity. Soon leaves began to wither and fall, the grass shriveled and turned brown, the earth dried and crusted. Wells ran dry. The streams stopped. It still did not stop. For days the hot, evil breath blew throughout the valley.

"It's the wicked witch," Mrs. Cotter told the villagers. "I knew it would happen. You have upset her."

"Indeed," chided Mrs. Crowe. "You should have listened to us, then none of this would have happened. Things were bad enough and now you've made them worse. All this nonsense about plants and leaving the valley."

"What are we to do?" the people asked. "If this continues, we will have no water at all. We will surely die."

The yellow man listened to their grumbling, but would not give in.

"We must go to the mountains and bring back snow. We will use that for water until the wind passes."

"Up to the mountains indeed," someone said to the other villagers. "It would be a full day's journey just to reach the snow, and another day back. Then how long would it last? There is a simpler answer. Destroy the plants and send the yellow man packing. Who asked him to come here anyway? Once he's gone, the witch will leave us alone again."

"You asked for me," the yellow man answered, to the puzzlement of the crowd. Without a further word, he gathered some buckets and started toward the mountains. Then, one or two others followed,

71

Mrs. Miller, and some of the young women and their husbands. The children thought it more a game than a chore, so they joined in. More followed until there was a small parade of people carrying buckets and pots up the mountain.

Those who remained looked angrily at the Mayor. This was not something that could be easily dealt with because there was no precedent for him to be guided by, not that there could ever have been a precedent, since things had always been the same in the valley, and the only one who could have set a precedent would have to have been himself, since he was the only mayor they ever had, and, therefore, not having a precedent to guide him was not something that could be easily dealt with. So the Mayor picked up a bucket and ran toward the mountain, thereby setting a precedent.

When the voyagers returned to the valley in two days, the wind still blew hot and dry. They watered their plants and tended their own needs. Then they shared what was left over with those who had refused to go up the mountain, but it was only enough for them to drink. After a night's rest the procession up the mountain began again the following morning. Four times they made the trip and back. Still the hot wind blew strong. When they returned from their fifth trip, the wind had ended. The wicked witch, totally exhausted from having blown the evil wind so long, collapsed on the floor of her hut in a dead faint. Lucifer walked over to the sleeping witch, stretched lazily, and went to sleep alongside her.

III

Once again, there was water in the valley. The creeks began to flow, the wells filled and the grass turned green. Life returned to normal as the people went about their daily chores.

As the weeks passed the special plants, carefully tended according to directions, began to grow bigger and bigger. The people who cared for them had even taken to singing and whistling. Their children were even allowed to play during the week. They lived in a kind of happy anticipation of what was to come.

All this greatly upset the more serious villagers. They felt no good could come from all this frivolity. If the seed growers really thought they were going through the frightful forest they had better take things more seriously too. The disapproving villagers said this as they cast fearful glances over their left shoulders.

In the witch's hut, the witch stirred from her exhausted sleep. She rose and walked over to the window. She squinted her eyes to focus sharply on the distant valley. It was normal again. She cocked her ears to listen closely. She heard singing. At first the sound puzzled her for she hadn't heard it in endless years. Then she grew angry. She flew into a fit of rage, shrieking and pulling at her hair. Lucifer, startled by the witch's outburst, spit and catapulted into the air, all four feet at once, then cowered in a corner complaining menacingly.

When her temper finally subsided, the witch returned to the window lost in deep and malicious thought. The cat, as if knowing that the storm was over and that more evil scheming was afoot, pranced over to her and leaped into her arms. The witch petted her with long, slow strokes.

"What now, my lovely? I'm afraid we slept too long. So their plants have grown have they? Well I may not be able to destroy them, but THEY can. Tonight they will blossom and blossoms smell nice, don't they, my pretty?"

Lucifer purred in response. The witch left the window and walked to her cupboard. She glanced quickly at several different bottles and jars until she found the one she was looking for.

"Yes," she hissed, "their blossoms will smell good enough to eat."

Once again she began to laugh, quietly at first but louder and louder as her plan came to life in her mind until she shrieked with delight. With the bottle in hand, she leaped from the window and flew straight to the valley. While the people slept, she put a drop from the bottle in each flower of all the special plants. When she was done, she returned to her vigil by the window.

The following morning as the townspeople set out to do their work, they were greeted with the smell of a strange, sweet perfume in the air. The news spread from house to house until everyone was outside sniffing the air. "It's the flowers from the yellow man's plants," they said. The smell was enchanting, captivating. Even those who hadn't grown them came over to get a closer smell.

"Why they almost smell good enough to eat," someone else said.

The thought provoked the temptation, and one of the young

boys picked a flower from his plant and gulped it down. The others gazed at him in surprise.

"After all, people don't eat flowers," remarked the mayor.

It had no particular taste at all, but a strange sensation came over the boy. Soon he broke out with a foolish giggle which he couldn't seem to control. Not that he wanted to. Then he began to bounce as if he were imitating some silly rabbit. The people watched in awe as he bounced higher and higher until he rose higher than the trees. It was as if the earth were made of rubber. Some adults began to stamp on the ground, cautiously, to see if it had somehow changed. But it hadn't. While they watched the bouncing boy, they were startled by another giggling, bouncing boy behind them, then another and another. They had each gone to their own plants and eaten the flowers. The sight of all these bouncing boys was certainly a funny one. When one of the adults ate a flower from his plant and started bouncing, the villagers roared with laughter. Even older people started eating their flowers then bounced along with the others. But their legs were not as strong so they wobbled when they landed and even wobbled in the air to the delight of the onlookers. Everywhere people started eating the flowers.

Mrs. Crowe looked on with disgust. "Act your age," she told the adults. "And you children get about your chores. All this nonsense! What has become of us?"

But no one listened. When the effects of one flower began to wear off, they returned to their plants and ate another.

From nowhere, the yellow man suddenly appeared. "You must not eat the flowers. If you eat them, the plants will not bear fruit."

Some who had been tempted to join the others were stopped short. They had waited this long, they felt, so they could wait a little longer. Others were tired of waiting, tired of tending their special plants, so they paid no heed.

After a short while a peculiar thing happened. Those who had not grown plants, wanting to join in with the bouncing people, asked if they might eat the flowers anyhow. The delighted bouncers readily agreed but when those who had not grown plants ate the blossoms, nothing happened. Not a bounce, not a stir. When the bouncers finished all their own flowers, without asking they went to pluck the others' flowers. However try as they might they could not do so.

Either the plants were too strong or the bouncers had grown too weak from bouncing but they could not pluck the other villagers' flowers.

A gentle breeze blew over the valley and carried away with it the captivating smell of the flowers. All the bouncing ended as the golden sun sank into the horizon.

Lucifer purred in the witch's arms.

"Wasn't that lovely, my pet? There's still time."

Night came to the valley.

IV

At long last, fruit appeared on the plants, then ripened. The time had come. The yellow man called the people together to prepare them for the journey.

"At the rising of the sun, we will leave on our journey to the wonderful land I told you about. Only those who have tended their plants may make the journey because only they will have the fruit which will be our food. You need not be afraid of the forest or the witch if you have it for it will make you strong. You must leave everything else behind, take nothing with you except the fruit. That is all you will need."

The villagers had so many questions but actually the instructions were quite clear. They returned to their homes hardly able to sleep for all the excitement that filled their heads.

When the first golden rays of the sun filled the valley, all the people gathered in the square. Each one who was to make the journey carried a sack filled with his fruit. Everyone was there: the Mayor, Mrs. Cotter with her knitting, indeed Mrs. Crowe, Mrs. Miller, and the yellow man. Everyone had come, either to leave or to see the others off on their journey. At the last moment even some of those who could go decided against it. They would not leave their relatives or friends behind. They could not leave their homes or possessions. They were afraid of the frightful forest or the wicked witch.

"It is time," said the yellow man.

With that, the villagers parted company. Those who were going made their farewells and started toward the forest.

"What about us?" asked Mrs. Cotter.

"Indeed, what about us?" repeated Mrs. Crowe.

The yellow man stopped and turned to the remaining villagers. He reached into his pocket and pulled out a handful of seeds.

"You must try again," he said, leaving enough seeds so that each person would have one.

"Who will be here to help us if you go away?"

"I will send someone."

The voyagers then entered the frightful forest.

V

The witch watched the proceedings from her window. "How dare they enter my forest. No matter, they'll be dancing a different tune before long."

The procession of voyagers led by the yellow man were well into the forest when they arrived at a clearing. The ground here was covered so densely with rocks that no tree or brush could grow. Without stopping they continued over them.

"Come my lovely," snickered the witch as she clutched Lucifer in her hands, "we must give our travelers a warm welcome." Then she flew down to the clearing.

As she stood there watching, she began to stroke Lucifer harder and harder. The cat's fur stood on end and began to spark. The harder she stroked, the more sparks flew from the cat until her hand was covered with sparks like a thousand, small lightning bolts. She then reached down and touched the rocks. The sparks traveled from her hand to the rocks and spread rapidly over them until they all sparkled and crackled.

The travelers stopped when they saw what was happening. Then they felt the heat of the rocks burning through their shoes and scorching their feet. They began to jump and hop in a vain attempt to avoid the pain. They were about to run back home when the yellow man cried out to them, "Eat some of the fruit." Quickly the people reached into their bags and began eating the fruit. At first they felt nothing at all, then a warm comfortable feeling filled their bodies. The warmth caused them to perspire. They perspired as they never had in their lives until water poured from them as from a fountain. The water from their bodies cooled the rocks so that they were once again able to continue their journey.

The wicked witch screamed furiously. She had never been beaten before. Not ever! Who was this golden man? He must not succeed. She must scare these villagers like she had never done before. They must not defy her or she would have no power over anyone any more.

She leaped up into the sky circling higher and higher until she was lost in some dark, black clouds. The voyagers saw her flight and became frightened. They stopped and looked over their left shoulders to where she had gone. Suddenly, there emerged from the clouds a monster, hideous beyond all imagination. It was a huge, incredibly huge dragon with three grotesque heads. One was that of a cat with a long, black tongue that screamed a hideous cry. Another head was of a huge, mad dog growling and snapping while foam dripped from its mouth. The third was that of the witch herself cackling and shrieking like some enormous wild bird. The voyagers were transfixed with terror as the hideous monster swooped down toward them.

"Eat the rest of the fruit," shouted the yellow man, barely audible amid the terrifying sounds descending on them. Frantically, they did as they were told.

It was a child who first showed the effects of the strange food this time. He looked up at the swooping monster and strangely, he began to laugh. The sight of the little boy laughing at such a frightful monster was so unexpected, so ridiculous, the others began to laugh. The monster reached the child first and reared up in all its awful fury, snapping and shrieking with every last ounce of its strength. Still the child laughed. The other children raced to see the ridiculous monster up close, and they, too, began laughing. The sight was too much for the voyagers. Peals of laughter bellowed out from the crowd until it grew so loud that it completely overcame the noise of the monster. Laughter filled the frightful forest echoing through the trees, over the rocks, and back into the valley where the remaining villagers listened and wondered.

In a puff of smoke, the witch disappeared. Behind the spot where she was standing stretched an endless vision of the most beautiful enchanted land they had ever dreamed. The voyage was over.

THE BEST CHRISTMAS GIFT OF ALL: A STORY OF SANTA AND THE CHRIST CHILD

It was a bad winter. A cold, hard and bitter winter. It was the month of December, almost Christmas, but there was no merriment. True, the stores were decorated in their Christmas finery; there were garlands and trees and pretty Christmas lights, but there were no shoppers or hardly any. On every city corner there were the usual Santa pots suspended from tripods but the Santas, who greeted shoppers with their ringing bells, were missing. Even the Salvation Army bands that had braved many a winter storm were gone. It was not because of the snow or the cold in that winter of 1918. It was the flu.

In an orphanage outside of New York City there lived three brothers. Francis, the oldest, was twelve, almost thirteen years old. Thomas was eleven and Little John was eight. They called him Little John not just because he was the youngest but because he was little and frail. When the epidemic was at its peak their mother died and a month later their father. Since they had no relatives they were taken to the orphanage where the good sisters took them in.

It was Christmas eve. All the children had just finished eating and were gathered in the large living room decorating the tree. There was a big, warm fire in the fireplace and the room was filled with sounds of popping corn and Christmas carols. The door opened and Sister Gertrude whisked in clapping her hands very officiously. "Hurry children. Finish the tree and drink your hot chocolate. We must all be in our beds fast asleep before Santa comes." The children hurriedly finished and were hustled off to bed.

Just before midnight everyone was asleep. The house was quiet except for the far off sound of the nuns singing in the chapel preparing for midnight mass. Francis quietly slipped out of bed and woke his brother Thomas. In a very soft voice he said, "Now I'll prove to you that there's no Santa Claus. We'll go downstairs and wait. You'll see. He won't come." The whispering woke Little John. "Where are you going?" he asked when he saw his brothers tiptoeing to the door. "You're going to see Santa Claus. I want to come too. I have something special I want to ask him."

"You can't come. You're too small. Besides you're sick with a bad cold and Sister Gertrude said you might get the flu."

Little John started to cry and then cough.

Thomas broke in. "We'd better take him along or he'll wake everybody up."

Not wanting to start a commotion, realizing that Little John was not the type to easily give in, Francis finally consented. "Well Okay, but bundle up." When all three boys had put on their bathrobes they sneaked downstairs. They entered the living room and quietly closed the big door behind them. The fire in the fireplace was almost

80

completely out so there was a chill in the room. They walked over to the drapes that covered the window and slipped behind them.

"Now we'll wait here where we can see," said Francis.

"I'm cold," complained Little John shivering a bit. "My hands are cold and my feet too."

"I told you not to come. Why don't you go upstairs to bed?"

"No. I have something special I want to ask Santa Claus," he said, stifling a cough.

"Then be quiet and stop complaining."

The time went by slowly. First midnight, then one and two. The grandfather clock just struck three when Thomas noticed a bright shooting star in the sky.

"Look," he shouted. "Look at that star," pointing out the window. Francis searched the sky until he too saw the star. Little John who had fallen asleep woke up and rubbed the sleep from his eyes.

"No. It's a comet," Francis said. "See how it moves across the sky." The boys watched it zigzag across the night sky descending faster and faster. It was getting closer but they could not see it well because their breathing had frosted the window. Francis opened the window to get a better view. The cold night air blew harshly into the room setting the drapes behind them flapping. It chilled Little John and made him shiver more but he coughed quietly under his breath so that his brothers wouldn't send him away.

"It's not a comet," said Thomas. "It's Santa Claus."

Coming quickly down toward the orphanage was a beautiful, shiny white and gold sleigh led by eight white reindeer. There at the reins was none other than St. Nicholas himself. He brought the sleigh to a halt just below the window where the boys peeked out. He grabbed hold of one of his bags and with a mighty leap jumped all the way to the rooftop.

When he started down the chimney the boys drew the drapes tight so that he wouldn't see them hiding. The moment he landed Santa hurried over to the tree and began putting his packages beneath it.

The boys watched quietly, holding the drapes open just enough so they could see what he was doing. But the cold air, caught behind the drapes, was too much for Little John who broke out into a violent coughing fit.

When Santa heard the noise he called out, "Who's there?"

"It's us," said Francis as the three boys stepped out from behind the curtain.

"Well now, what are you doing here? You boys should be in bed asleep."

"We wanted to wait up to see if you were really coming." Francis always spoke for the three.

"Well, why wouldn't I? It's Christmas eve, isn't it?"

"Yes, but you see, Santa," stammered Francis, "I didn't think you were real."

"Not real?" he laughed, "not real." He almost doubled over in hysterics. "Do you think you're getting too old for me, Francis? Come here and see if I'm real."

After the boys had convinced themselves that he was indeed real by touching and poking him and pulling his beard, Santa said, "I suppose now you're wondering what I brought you for Christmas? But tell me first, what you wanted."

"I know what I want," said Thomas. "More than anything else I want a sled."

"A sled, is it now? And you Francis, what did you want?"

"I haven't given it much thought," he answered, "but I guess I would like a pair of ice skates."

"And you, Little John. What is it you would like for Christmas?"

Little John stood there shivering from fright and cold. "Oh Santa! I want something special for Christmas. I want my mommy."

"Well now," said Santa stroking his white beard. "Well, well now," he kept repeating, scratching his nose with his hand. "I have a surprise for all three of you. I am going to give you the best Christmas gift of all."

"What is it, Santa? What is it?" asked Thomas and Little John.

"Oh, I don't have it here, but I'll take you with me to where it is. Do you want to come?"

"Yes. Yes. Yes," they replied. Even Francis lost his reserve.

"Then bundle yourselves up," Santa said. The boys tied their bathrobes tighter. "Hold round my neck, Francis." He grabbed hold of Thomas and Little John, one under each arm, and jumped out the window to his sleigh. The boys settled themselves in the back amidst bags and bags of toys. In a flash they were off.

Up into the night sky they flew as quickly as a comet. They

traveled from city to city, town to town, waiting in the sleigh while Santa made his deliveries. When they grew restless and asked about their gift, Santa would just reply "Soon," and continue on. Finally, Francis asked if they might get off to stretch their legs a bit. The sleigh came down in a valley. When the boys had gotten off, Santa said to them, "I'll be back shortly. Don't wander off too far." With that he and his sleigh and his reindeer took off again into the sky.

The night air was bitter cold and it wasn't long before Little John began to complain, "My hands are cold and my feet too." Then he began to cough and cough badly.

"Maybe we can find some place to warm up," said Francis. So the boys began walking in search of a shelter. Not too far away they came to a well where a young boy was drawing water.

"Hello" Francis greeted him.

"Hello."

"Who are you?"

"I am Jude."

"My name is Francis and this is my brother Thomas and my brother Little John. I wonder if you could help us. Little John is cold and sick. Do you know where we can go to warm him up?"

"There is a physician who lives near here. He has all kinds of wonderful medicines. Go to him. I am sure he has something that can make your brother well again."

So Jude left his bucket to lead the three boys to the house of the physician which was at the edge of a small village.

"What have we here," said the physician who answered the knock at his door. "Four night travelers. What is it you want?"

"My brother is sick," said Francis. "He's very cold and he coughs a lot. Do you have something you can give him?"

"Cold, eh? Sick, eh? Coughs you say? Well, I have just the thing." He went to a shelf and returned with a small bottle. "It is a special ointment from the East. I purchased it from a trader for quite a sum of money. Rub it on his body and he will warm up immediately."

"May I have some sir?" asked Francis.

"Have some? You mean free? No, I can't do that. It cost me very much money to buy it. But there is just a little left now, just enough for a little boy his size." He pointed to Little John. "You may buy what's left for one gold coin."

"But we have no money," Francis pleaded.

"Well, see to that yourselves. Come back with the money and I will give you the oil."

The boys walked away saddened. "Where will we get the money?" asked Thomas.

"I know!" Jude replied. "There have been many caravans traveling through the village lately. Sometimes when I water the animals, they give me money. Maybe we can do that."

So the boys hurried into the village. Little John began coughing more—and harder. "My hands are cold and my feet too," he complained.

"What are we going to do with you?" cried Francis. "You're so sick you wont be able to work either."

"There's a stable behind the inn here," said Jude. "We can leave your brother there until we earn the money."

"Good," agreed Francis to the suggestion. At least he wouldn't have to listen to Little John's coughing or complaining.

The boys walked behind the inn to the stable. It was dark and cold and smelled heavily of animals. They told Little John to lay down in a corner and covered him with hay to keep him warm. Groping their way out they could hear him sneezing and coughing. "We'll have to get the money soon," said Francis.

As the boys entered the village a large caravan of camels was approaching the Inn. Jude ran over to the merchant.

"Sir," he cried, "you have many camels and you must have come a long way. If you'd like, my friends and I will water your animals and bed them for the night."

"Do that," the merchant replied, "and when you have finished come to me in the Inn and I will pay you well."

So the boys led the camels to the well where they hauled water for what seemed like hours. When the animals had drunk their fill, the boys bedded them down and hastened to the Inn.

As they approached the door they saw, waiting there, a man and a beautiful young woman seated astride a donkey. The Innkeeper came to the door, "Good travelers, what is it you want?" he asked.

"A room, Innkeeper," said the man. "My wife and I have been traveling long and we are tired."

"We have no more rooms."

"There are no more inns," the traveler replied. "The others are all filled. As you can see, my wife is heavy with child and we must rest."

"I'm sorry. We have no more rooms," he said, closing the door.

The scene was indeed a sad one and the boys looked on helplessly. Jude then slowly approached the stranger, "Sir, there is a place where you may spend the night with your wife. It is just a stable but it is not so bad or as cold as outdoors."

The man looked thoughtfully at the boy, then turned to his wife. "I can go no further," she replied. "Yes, Joseph."

"Show us," he said and the boys led them to the stable where Little John was sleeping.

Once again as they entered the dark stable the air was cold and heavy with the smell of animals. The man Joseph said to his wife, "I will make it cleaner then go and look for an inn for the morrow."

The woman waited at the door while her husband prepared a place for her. Inside, Little John stirred and coughed. The sound brought the boys back to their plight.

"We must hurry," remembered Francis, "and buy the ointment for Little John." So back they went to the inn to see the merchant. The merchant was so pleased to be relieved of an unpleasant burden that he gave each of the boys a gold coin.

They hurried then to the physician and bought the ointment. While they were making their way back through the village Jude suddenly stopped in front of the lamp maker's shop. "The traveler's wife will be alone with Little John in the dark stable. Perhaps we can bring them a lamp that will give them light and some heat."

"Yes, but we must hurry," said Francis.

The lamp maker showed them his largest and best lamp. "Bright enough to light a village—and feel the heat it gives. Fit for a king."

"How much?" Jude asked.

"How much have you?" questioned the merchant.

"I have a gold coin and so do my friends."

"Two gold coins exactly. Just the price."

They gave the merchant the money and hurried to the stable with the lamp and the physician's ointment.

The merchant spoke truly. The lamp indeed lit the entire stable. The woman was asleep on the hay. "Look," said Thomas to Francis as he held the lamp close to her, "doesn't she look like mother?"

"She does. In a way, I guess she does."

"Quiet, we must not disturb her," said Jude who then placed the lamp on the stone floor near her.

Francis walked over to Little John who was sleeping and woke him up. "Take this oil now and do what the doctor said. Put it all over your body, then you'll be warm in no time." Little John was still heavy with sleep and began rubbing his eyes against the light in the stable.

At that moment Jude called to Francis. "The air is very heavy with animals. Let us surprise the woman. There are some roots nearby that, when they are burned, fill the air with a beautiful perfume. Let's go and collect some."

Francis looked at Little John who was just getting up. He'd be all right for a little while longer. The three boys hurried out into the night to gather the roots. While they were busily digging for them in the fields, a strange noise began to fill the night. They strained their ears to hear it at first, but it became louder and louder. It was singing. It was like the sound of the sisters singing in chapel. It was not one voice, nor even a hundred but thousands. It filled the night sky with its sweetness. It hummed through the trees and flowed over the valley, a magnificent symphony of voices. Then, slowly it faded and passed away.

"What a strange night this is." Jude had broken the silence. When the boys returned to the stable Little John was asleep but the woman was awake and seated. She was bathed in the golden glow of the lamp they had brought. When she saw the boys she smiled at them and pointed to the manger. There, lying on the hay, they saw a babe; tiny and small its body gleamed in the lamp light. While Francis and Thomas stared at the child, Jude put the roots on the lamp. Soon a sweet odor of perfume filled the stable. They were still staring when the sound of sleigh bells approached outside.

"It's Santa," cried Thomas and he and Francis ran outside to greet him. Sure enough, there was Santa and his sleigh and reindeer.

Excitedly, the boys told him all that had happened since he'd left them. They told him about their friend Jude, then about the physician, the merchant and his camels, the traveling couple, the strange night music and the baby. They were still talking when Santa interrupted them. "I see you've been having a busy night. Well, from all that you've told me about all you've done, I think you're ready to know what is the best Christmas gift of all. The best Christmas gift of all," he said solemnly, "is not getting what you want but giving to someone who needs. I see that you've learned that already tonight. So now, let me ask you again. What would you like for Christmas?"

He looked first at Thomas who was repeating to himself the wisdom Santa had just told them, '. . . not getting what you want but giving to someone who needs.' He thought of the sled but that's what he wanted. '. . . someone who needs.' He thought then of his brother Little John. "Santa! Little John is always cold and sick. What I would like for Christmas is for him not to be cold and sick any more."

"And you Francis. What do you want?"

Francis thought of the ice skates that he really wanted so desperately. But that wouldn't be the best gift. He then thought of Little John cold and coughing and remembered what his frail brother wanted from Santa. "Santa, could you please give Little John my mother?"

Without saying another word Santa pointed to the stable window. The two brothers walked over and looked inside. There within, Little John, having been roused from sleep again was walking to the manger rubbing his eyes. The sound of the child crying filled the air. Little John walked to the manger and looked in wonder at the tiny child laying there. He then reached in and touched the baby's hands. They were cold like his. He then touched the baby's feet. They too were cold like his. He reached into the pocket of his bathrobe and took out the jar of ointment. He rubbed some on the baby's hands and then his feet. The oil that was left he rubbed on the baby's body. Within moments the child stopped crying and fell asleep. The beautiful lady smiled then stretched out her arms to Little John. He climbed up on her lap. She enfolded him in her arms and he fell asleep.

Santa walked up behind the two brothers still gazing through the stable window. He placed his two big arms around them and in a voice just above a whisper he said, "This night you boys have learned wisdom. You did not ask, you gave. What you gave were the most precious gifts of all—gold, frankincense and myrrh."

The first rays of dawn broke over the horizon. In a bound Santa lifted the boys onto his sleigh and off they went into the early morning sky. The brothers, tired out from the long night and the hard work, curled up in the back of the sleigh, covered themselves with the now empty sacks and soon fell fast asleep.

Sister Gertrude came walking down the stairs rubbing her hands because of the morning chill. When she opened the door to the living room, a bitter cold wind blew hard against her. "Mercy sakes," she cried, "someone must have left the window open." She walked to the window where the wind billowed out the drapes. When she parted them she gave a startled cry. There were the brothers all huddled on the floor. "Sweet mother of mercy, holy mother of God!" she cried. "They must be frozen to death!" She ran to the stairs and cried out to the other Sisters for help. "Sisters, hurry. Come quickly. We must get the children to their beds. Bring blankets. Call the Doctor. Boil water."

It was late in the afternoon when Francis awoke. For a moment he thought he was still in the sleigh. Then he saw Sister Gertrude sitting in her rocking chair beside his bed with her eyes closed devoutly praying her rosary.

"Sister, wait till I tell you what happened," he said excitedly. His words at first startled the nun who looked at him as if he were Lazarus come back from the dead. Francis moved to get out of bed but Sister Gertrude quickly got up and stopped him.

"Thank God. Thank heavens. You mustn't get out of bed. The doctor forbids it. You must rest."

But Francis was too excited; he had so much to tell she couldn't stop him from talking. She begged him to be quiet for fear he'd wake his brother Thomas, asleep in the next bed but his words kept pouring out in endless profusion. At first the nun was too overcome to listen but as he continued his tale, she sat up in her rocking chair in rapt attention. And so his story unfolded: the ride with Santa; the boy Jude and the physician; the two travelers, the one a beautiful lady. Each detail flowed out and was relived again. He told of watering the camels; hurrying for the ointment; buying the lantern; digging for roots in the field, hearing the beautiful music. Then coming back to the stable and finding the infant. And Little John giving his own ointment to the baby before cuddling up in the beautiful lady's arms.

This last recollection of Little John made Francis suddenly stop his story. He looked at Thomas' bed where his brother lay sleeping. He turned to Little John's bed. It was empty.

"Little John," he cried, "where's Little John?"

"You must rest now. Too much excitement. The doctor will be angry." Sister Gertrude stood nervously clutching her beads.

"Sister, where is he? Where's Little John?"

"He's not here," she whispered.

The scene suddenly came back to him. The beautiful lady reaching out to Little John then taking him in her arms—then Santa hurrying him and Thomas onto the sleigh. The thought suddenly struck him. Little John was not on the sleigh. They had left him at the stable.

"Where is he, sister?" he asked again. "Where's my brother?"

Sister Gertrude swallowed deeply searching for breath. She gazed up to the ceiling lifting her head in a vain attempt to hold back the tears.

"He's gone away," she choked as she walked to the window, not wanting Francis to see her face.

The voice behind her changed. It was no longer the voice of a child. "I know," he said. "I know now. Little John got the best Christmas gift of all."

Appendix

THE WART PRINCESS

It would appear from the Gospel passage that it is better not to cast out an evil spirit. (Matthew 12:43-45) This fairy tale is an explanation of how "the seven spirits more evil than the first" come to inhabit one's house. The moral is that one's purpose is what is important in expelling a demon. To do so for your own sake is to open the door to even greater difficulties. Selfishness should never be the motive even for an apparent good. To want to lose weight or give up smoking with only yourself as the motive is rarely sufficient to sustain the effort. It can also cause a person to become impatient or tyrannical toward one's spouse, children or friends. One expels demons for the sake of the kingdom. I stop smoking because my family needs me. I eat less because there are hungry people in the world. Then, when the evil spirit is cast out, Jesus fills the vacuum.

JOHNNY CRAB AND THE LEPRECHAUN

Johnny Crab and the Leprechaun is a tale whose theme is the right to life or its opposite, abortion, infanticide, euthanasia.

The baseball game is the game of life. Each player not allowed to participate or put out of the game is thru symbol excluded from life.

Sammy the Shrimp, Dodo Dennis, Silly Sally and Lightning Louis represent the stages of life that society has put in jeopardy. Johnny Crab is placed in their position by the contests the Leprechaun puts him through.

Sammy the Shrimp—symbolizes the fetus struggling for emergence (life). Mr. Harump symbolizes either the mother or society not wanting to be upset. He is given three hours (the first trimester) to win the contest. Having failed to do so he kicks over the chair, an omen of what can happen in the future.

Dodo Dennis—symbolizes the profoundly retarded or emotionally disturbed. Their inability to communicate imperils their existence and the contest is prematurely ended even though "the right one" hasn't come along yet.

Silly Sally—symbolizes handicapped people whose ways are not the "right" ways. Sometimes called "the ninth-hour child" they show Johnny Crab that he is the misfit in their world.

Lightning Louie—symbolizes our old people, who after having run the race and received the awards of life that now weigh heavily on them must compete with the untried and untired in order to win the final contest.

Johnny Crab having walked in another's shoes offers final hope for victory.

THE PEASANT AND THE PRINCESS

Although the two Gospel passages are not related in the Biblical text, I have drawn them together in this tale to solve a dilemma. The first account of the laborers in the vineyard was as bitter a pill to swallow (pardon the analogy) for the Jews of Jesus' time as it is for many people today. Somehow this parable still offends our sense of justice. Let me cite an example. I once worked in an office where quite unexpectedly new employees were given a starting salary equal to those who had been working for two and three years. When the experienced employees began to complain, the employer posted this parable on the employees' bulletin board. I leave the reaction to your imagination. Hence, the dilemma. Does the second parable provide a solution? Note well that the fairy tale is not a case of The Lady *Or* The Tiger, but The Peasant *And* The Princess.

THE YELLOW MAN

The village in the valley is a vision of this world with its difficulties, hopes, fears and superstitions. It is a symbol of unredeemed mankind awaiting the promised one—"you asked for me."

The bridegroom comes to prepare the people for salvation. Two elements essential for salvation are introduced: one's own responsibility and the journey with others.

1) One's own responsibility: Each is given his own seed (salvation is a free gift of God to everyone) and he must tend to it himself. One cannot take another's—"when those who had not grown plants ate the blossoms nothing happened," "they could not pluck the other villagers' flowers."

2) Social responsibility: There was need for working together to water the plants and give mutual support in the frightful forest.

The fruit of the plant is a symbol of the Eucharist which is called "food for pilgrims." Nothing else is needed, neither walking stick, nor sandal for this journey. God will provide.

The encounter with the wicked witch is the ultimate fear —death. But death has lost its victory and is ludicrous to those who walk in faith.

The wise virgins enter with the bridegroom. Still there is hope for the foolish ones to whom the invitation is again extended, "I will send someone," the Holy Spirit.

JOHN R. AURELIO, a Catholic priest of the diocese of Buffalo, is spiritual director at Christ the King Seminary, East Aurora, NY, and author of many popular books, including *Fables for God's People*, *Mosquitoes in Paradise*, *The Garden of Life*, *Skipping Stones*, and most recently *Myth Man: A Storyteller's Jesus*, which has been praised as "a life of Christ for the 90s."